Securing Microsoft Terminal Services
First Edition

Author:
Roddy Rodstein, CISSP, MCSE, LPI, CEH, CCA

Limits of Liability and Disclaimer of Warranty

This publication contains information protected by copyright. This book may not be duplicated in any way without the express written consent of the publisher, except in the form of brief excerpts or quotations for the purpose of review. The information contained herein is for the personal use of the reader and may not be incorporated in any commercial programs, other books, databases, or any kind of software without the written consent of the publisher. Making copies of this book or any portion for any purpose other than your own is a violation of United States copyright laws.

Warning and Disclaimer

Every effort has been made to make this book as complete and as accurate as possible, but no warranty or fitness is implied. The information provided is on an "as is" basis. The authors and the publisher shall have neither liability nor responsibility to any person or entity with respect to any loss or damages arising from the information contained in this book. The information found in this document was gathered from many different sources in the computing world. It is provided for informational purposes only. Use common sense in applying these concepts and tips. Screen shots may vary from environment to environment. Please verify correctness and applicability in a test environment first and then deploy to your production environment(s).

Trademarks

Trademarked names appear throughout this book. Rather than listing the names and entities that own the trademarks or include a trademark symbol with each mention of the trademark name, the publisher states that he is using the name for editorial purposes only and to the benefit of the trademark owner, with no intention of infringing upon that trademark.

Dedication

This book is dedicated to my mother, Marcia Haenle, who is living proof that life just keeps getting better and better.

—Roddy

About the Author

Roddy Rodstein (CISSP, MCSE, LPI, CEH, CCA) is an Enterprise Systems Engineer currently employed at Citrix Systems. He has over 10 years experience in the IT industry, spending the last five with Citrix Systems, Inc. Before Citrix, Roddy successfully established, owned, and operated an IT consulting business that specialized in server based computing and remote access solutions. In 2000, Roddy wrote and published the *Citrix CCA MetaFrame 1.8 for Windows Exam Cram* (ISBN: 1576109453). Once at Citrix, he followed with several of the "in the Box" series e-Books, starting with *Nfuse Elite in a Box*, *MetaFrame Secure Access Manager in a Box*, *MetaFrame Presentation Server for UNIX in a Box*, and recently *Citrix Smart Access in a Box*. Roddy is a regular speaker and tutorial presenter at West Cost IT events, Citrix iForum, Citrix Summit and BriForum.

Acknowledgments

Thanks to all the people in my life who have been patient with me while I worked on this project. A special thanks also to Doug Brown of DABCC.COM for all of his help in making this book possible, Brad Tompkins for taking the time to read multiple revisions of the book and providing his invaluable input and to Greyson Mitchem for his support.

—Roddy

As the reader of my book, you are my most important critic. I really value your opinion and would like to understand your security challenges, what we can do better in security areas, and what areas you'd like to see me write about.

I welcome your comments! Please feel free to email me directly or visit my web site to let me know what you did or didn't like about this book as well as what I can do to make the next edition of this book better.

When you write, please be sure to include this book's title, your name, and your email address. I will carefully review your comments and get back with you as soon as possible.

Please stay tuned to http://www.vellity.com for the Securing Microsoft Terminal Services errata page, security articles, and whitepapers.

Email: roddy.rodstein@vellity.com
Web Site: http://www.vellity.com

Chapters at a Glance

Policies at a Glance

Table of Contents

Table of Contents

Preface

I would like to welcome you to the first edition of *Securing Microsoft Terminal Services*. This book was developed to provide architects, project managers, consultants, and network and security administrators with guidance in order to secure Terminal Server environments using widely adopted industry standards. My goal with this book is to share what I've learned first hand about how organizations successfully secure their Terminal Server environments. Beginning with Chapter 4, I introduce policies that follow established methodologies, standards, and guidelines that demonstrate how to plan, build, run, and monitor a Terminal Server environment from an information security and regulatory compliance perspective. When applicable, regulatory compliance will be addressed in each chapter to provide guidance on how to comply with regulatory mandates, such as Sarbanes-Oxley, Health Insurance Portability and Accountability (HIPAA) or Gramm-Leach-Bliley (GLB) regulations.

Spending the last five years at Citrix Systems as Senior Enterprise Systems Engineer supporting Enterprise, SME, and SMB customers has given me an amazing opportunity to learn first hand how organizations successfully secure their Terminal Server environments. After a short time in the field, I realized that there was no single document, whitepaper, or book that presents a holistic approach to securing a Terminal Server environment. I still hear the same questions over and over, "Is there a book or whitepaper that explains how to secure my Terminal Server environment?" These inquiries inspired me to write this book.

It is often said that information security is a process, not a product. The information security (InfoSec) community agrees that information security must do more than employ technical controls, such as a firewall or anti-virus software, to protect against threats from misappropriate system use, intruders, bugs, exploits, viruses and worms. The goal of this book is to demonstrate how Terminal Server fits within an organization's information security system, while identifying where and how to implement administrative and technical security controls. This book follows proven information security methodologies, leveraging widely adopted information technology management frameworks, standards, and guidelines that enable organizations of any size to maximize the return on investment (ROI) from IT and to achieve business objectives while significantly reducing risk. Beginning with Chapter 4, I will introduce example policies that map directly to security frameworks, standards, and guidelines such as ISO17799, CobIT, the National Security Agency (NSA) Guides, and Security Technical Implementation Guides (STIGS). The closing chapters will address compliance, monitoring, auditing, and conducting a vulnerability assessment.

The term "Enterprise" used throughout this book refers to organizations with multiple internal networks, diverse sets of PCs, numerous information systems and applications, various access requirements, and a diverse user population.

Chapter 1: Terminal Server and Enterprise Security

Chapter Overview:
This chapter begins with a high level overview of Terminal Server, Terminal Server security considerations, and an introduction to Enterprise Architecture. It continues with a brief introduction to the written policies in this book and concludes with a high level overview of the Control Frameworks and Management Standards that are referenced throughout this book. The goal of this chapter is to introduce Terminal Server in the context of an Enterprise Architecture and introduce Control Frameworks and Management Standards.

Terminal Server is the de facto Server Based Computing solution for Microsoft environments that offers organizations a cost effective way to centrally host, manage and secure Windows desktops, Windows applications and data. Terminal Server reduces complexity, enhances security, and simplifies regulatory compliance by moving applications and data from PCs to a centrally managed Terminal Server environment. Application access, application updates, operating system service packs, and security hotfixes are centrally managed on the Terminal Servers and not on each individual PC. The centralization of computing resources is called the Server Based Computing model.

Access to a Terminal Server environment is enabled by using a small piece of client software commonly referred to as the remote desktop client (RDC) or remote desktop protocol client (RDP). Terminal Server offers organizations a way to reduce the amount of client software supported on each PC from an entire desktop application portfolio to a single piece of client software, the RDC client. RDC is pre-installed on Microsoft operating systems and is widely available on non-Windows operating systems, such as Apple, Linux, and UNIX.

Server Based Computing offers inherent security advantages over other computing models by providing centralized control of the entire desktop environment (i.e., centralization of the Windows desktop environment, Windows applications, data and information, and centralization of network traffic). Server Based Computing, in conjunction with Enterprise Security Architecture design principles, offers extreme flexibility in implementing the appropriate security controls to protect internal or confidential applications and data. For example, one Terminal Server silo (a group of Terminal Servers) can be used to gain access to internal office productivity applications and data, while another Terminal Server silo can be used to access confidential financial or human resource applications and data. This flexibility allows organizations to implement the appropriate security controls based on the critically or sensitivity of an application or data. Access to applications and data from Terminal Servers can be logged and filtered via group membership with timestamps in order to provide non-repudiation. These capabilities provide a cost effective solution that allows organizations to secure their applications and data and to meet business objectives and regulatory mandates.

Terminal Services provide the flexibility for organizations to host a single application or an entire desktop application portfolio on one or many Terminal Servers. Desktop applications are installed, managed, and executed on Terminal Servers that sit as close as possible to the data, thereby shortening the distance data travels over the network and effectively centralizing network traffic and data management. Client sessions use the highly efficient RDP protocol to communicate to a Terminal Server, which in turn communicates directly to supporting information systems located on the same or adjacent network.

Server Based Computing has demonstrable security and performance advantages over other computing models because of the centralization of applications and network traffic. When a client-server application, such as a mail client, runs on a PC, it communicates directly to a mail server. This communication traverses the entire network from the PC all the way to the mail server. Client-server traffic characteristically uses substantially more bandwidth then RDP and requires a wide variety of open communication ports between workstations and servers, which increases the attack surface between networks.

Terminal Server users interact with applications and data from a virtualized Terminal Server desktop that is presented to end users via an RDP client. Terminal Server desktops are identical to PC desktops in appearance and functionality and can be displayed in full screen, predefined sizes, or a percentage of the local monitor. This shifts the security focus from PC desktops to the Terminal Server environment and supporting backend information systems.

Securing a Terminal Server environment presents challenges due in part to the characteristics of Server Based Computing because user sessions move from PCs to Terminal Servers. Terminal Servers are characteristically placed as close as possible to the data, in many cases on the same network as the data. This model moves the security controls from the PCs and their network to the Terminal Server desktop environment and the data center network. Because Terminal Servers might be located on the same network as supporting information systems, a compromised Terminal Server could be used as a hacking vector to other systems. This emphasizes the need to employ layered security controls through the Enterprise to effectively secure the Terminal Servers and supporting back-end systems. Security controls are employed using industry standard frameworks and standards to develop an Enterprise Architecture (EA). An Enterprise Architecture enables organizations to create an organizational wide blueprint that can be used to achieve business objectives, while maximizing the business value of information technology.

Organizations turn to Enterprise Architecture to understand how a Terminal Server solution fits with their entire information system. An Enterprise Architecture is a "blueprint" that describes an organization's strategic direction, business requirements, information technology portfolio, processes, and security measures used to implement and support technologies. An Enterprise Architecture is articulated in diagrams and written policies that define organizational standards and best practices to plan, build, run, and monitor technologies.

Enterprise Architecture has well defined principles and processes and an approach that generates a comprehensive, layered policy infrastructure used to communicate management's goals, principles, instructions, appropriate procedures, and response to laws and regulatory mandates. A policy infrastructure consists of written tier 1, tier 2, and tier 3 policies that encompass people, systems, data, and information. Policies are broken down into high level policies and lower level standards, procedures, baselines, and guidelines.

Written policies are either tier 1, tier 2, or tier 3. Tier 1 policies sit at the top of policy infrastructure addressing broad organizational wide issues, vision, and direction. Most organizations develop and support a dozen tier 1 policies. Tier 2 policies are typically vendor agnostic and describe high level business and technical requirements. Tier 3 policies are vendor, technology, and procedural specific.

Terminal Server policies typically fall within the layered policy infrastructure of the platform architecture domain, which is reviewed in Chapter 4. Platform architecture policies are the foundation used to manage the entire lifecycle of a Terminal Server environment.

Table 1.1 lists the security policies and chapters that are reviewed in this book.

Table 1.1

Policy	Explanation	Chapter
Platform Architecture Policy	A Platform Architecture Policy is a tier 2 policy that defines high level computing platform requirements.	Chapter 4
Network Architecture Policy	A Network Architecture Policy is a tier 2 policy that defines network architecture requirements and describes how information processing resources are interconnected.	Chapter 4
Data/Information Classification and Categorization Standard	A Data/Information Classification and Categorization Standard is a tier 2 policy that defines classifications and security	Chapter 4

	levels for all forms of data/information and information systems across the Enterprise.	
Terminal Server Application Software Policy	A Terminal Server Application Software Policy is a tier 3 policy that defines the application software life cycle for a Terminal Server environment.	Chapter 4
Terminal Server Anti-Virus Software Guidelines	A Terminal Server Anti-Virus Software Guidelines is a tier 3 policy that shows how an organization uses a guideline to suggest best practices in order to acquire, implement, and configure anti-virus software for Terminal Server.	Chapter 4
Change Management Policy	Change Management Policy is a tier 2 policy that defines the change management procedures for hardware, software, firmware, and documentation.	Chapter 4
Enterprise Security Policy	An Enterprise Security Policy is a tier 2 policy that is used to bridge a gap between technical and administrative security controls used to instruct employees and business partners on how to securely access systems and consume data securely.	Chapter 5
Risk Assessment Policy	A Risk Assessment Policy is a tier 2 policy that defines an organization's security Risk Assessment (RAs) strategy.	Chapter 5

IT Server Room Security Policy	An IT Server Room Security Policy is a tier 2 policy that defines the security controls employed to protect a server room against unauthorized access, environmental threats, and manmade disasters.	Chapter 6
Password Policy	A Password Policy is a tier 2 policy that defines a standard for creating strong passwords, the protection of those passwords, and the frequency of password changes.	Chapter 7
Windows Terminal Server Standards	Windows Terminal Server Standards is a tier 3 policy that defines organizational Terminal Server standards and requirements from a plan, build, run, and monitor perspective.	Chapter 8
Windows Server Security Policy	A Windows Server Security Policy is a tier 3 policy that defines an organization's Windows server security and minimum server standards.	Chapter 9
Terminal Server Installation Baseline	A Terminal Server Installation Baseline is a tier 3 policy that provides employees with an approved procedure to install Terminal Server.	Chapter 10
Terminal Server Security Baseline	A Terminal Server Security Baseline is a tier 3 policy that defines the process to implement security controls for a terminal Server environment.	Chapter 11

Software Restriction Policy Baseline	A Software Restriction Policy Baseline is a tier 3 policy that defines an organization's approved configuration standard for Microsoft Software Restriction Policies.	Chapter 12
Session Directory Configuration Baseline	A Session Directory Configuration Baseline is a tier 3 policy that defines an organization's approved installation and configuration standard for Microsoft Session Directory.	Chapter 13
Terminal Server Session Directory Group Policy Configuration Baseline	A Terminal Server Session Directory Group Policy Configuration Baseline is a tier 3 policy used to define an approved configuration standard for Terminal Servers that participate in a Terminal Server Session Directory environment.	Chapter 13
Terminal Server Network Load-Balancing Configuration Baseline	A Network Load-Balancing Configuration Baseline is a tier 3 policy that defines an approved installation and configuration standard for Microsoft Network Load-Balancing for Terminal Server.	Chapter 14
Log Management Policy	A Log Management Policy is a tier 2 policy that defines log management practices and requirements.	Chapter 16
Incident Response Policy	An Incident Response Policy is a tier 2 policy that defines how an organization responds to security incidents.	Chapter 17

Audit Vulnerability Scan Policy	An Audit Vulnerability Scan Policy is a tier 2 policy that defines the agreement to perform network security scanning.	Chapter 18

This section will review the Control Frameworks and Management Standards that are referenced throughout this book. I will highlight Cobit, ISO/IEC 17799, National Institute of Standards and Technology (NIST) Computer Security Division Publications, National Security Agency (NSA) Guides, and the Security Technical Implementation Guides (STIGS).

Regulatory compliance has managed to accomplish what age old, common sense arguments based on economics and efficiency could not: they have compelled organizations to consider and fund the development of strategies to manage and secure their information systems. There has always been a solid business case for information technology management based on cost-savings and risk reduction. Unfortunately, these arguments often fell on deaf ears, until Sarbanes-Oxley, Health Insurance Portability and Accountability (HIPAA) and Gramm-Leach-Bliley (GLB), and others re-focused attention on this need. Regulatory compliance helps move organizations from their current typically ad hoc security state to a recommended compliant state. Organizations turn to Control Frameworks and Management Standards to help develop strategies to reach a recommended compliant state.

Figure 1.1 shows current vs. recommended security state.

Figure 1.1

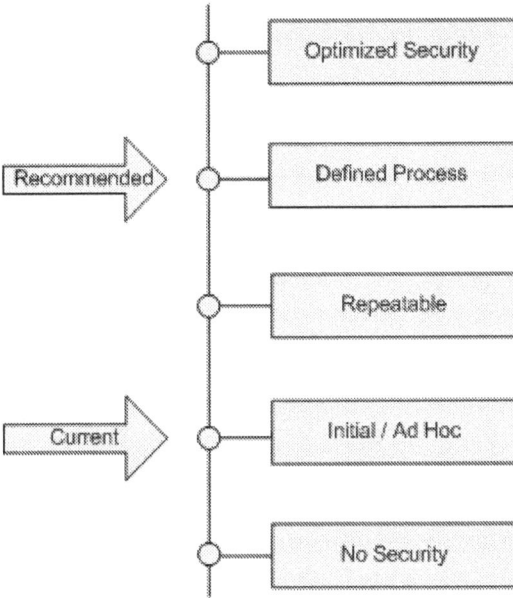

In terms of information security and compliance, there are many widely adopted frameworks, standards, and guidelines that provide recommendations and best practices on information security management, service management, and compliance. Typically, organizations mix and match frameworks and standards to meet their specific business objectives and regulatory needs. This strategy allows an organization to employ proven, widely adopted frameworks and standards in order to develop an Enterprise Architecture to manage and audit the entire life cycle of their technology investments.

Many frameworks and standards are developed by committees of volunteers from members of industry, governments, and the public. This methodology allows large groups of industry professionals to collaboratively develop, approve, and publish their work. An excellent example is the International Organization for Standardization (ISO), which has issued over 10,000 international standards. The International Organization for Standardization leverages more than 20,000 experts from all over the world who share in the development of ISO standards.

Control Frameworks and Management Standards share a common theme: they provide a comprehensive management layer around the entire life cycle of information technology.

CobIT

CobIT is a mature, control framework, first released in 1996 by the Information Systems Audit and Control Association (ISACA). Since its origin, it has evolved with a second edition in 1998, a third in 2000, and a fourth in November 2005. CobIT is maintained by the IT Governance Institute (ITGI) and Information Systems Audit and Control Association (ISACA). ISACA describes CobIT as a "framework and supporting toolset that allows managers to bridge the gap between control requirements, technical issues and business risks" (ref: ISACA). CobIT has become the de facto standard for auditors and Sarbanes-Oxley compliance, thereby significantly increasing its visibility and use. CobIT has been widely mapped against the "big three" standards: COSO, ITIL, and ISO 17799.

CobIT is comprised of six documents. List 1.2 shows the six documents.
- Management Guidelines
- Implementation ToolSet
- Executive Summary
- Framework
- Control Objectives
- Audit Guidelines

From a structural perspective, CobIT consists of a set of 215 Control Objectives for information technology, intended to enable auditing. The Control Objectives are used for guidance, in that they describe what should be accomplished.

CobIT can be downloaded at no cost from http://www.isaca.org/cobit/

ISO/IEC 17799

ISO/IEC 17799 is published by the International Organization for Standardization (ISO) and the International Electrotechnical Commission (IEC). ISO and the IEC are international standards organizations with members that include the standards bodies from many countries. ISO/IEC 17799 provides guidance for security policy, staff security awareness, business continuity planning, and legal requirements.

ISO/IEC 17799 was originally published by a government department in the United Kingdom as a Code of Practice (CoP) for Information Security. From there it was re-branded and published in 1995 as BS 7799 by the British Standards Institute (BSI). In December 2000, it was re-published as the ISO 17799 by ISO. In December 2005 it was revised and published as ISO/IEC 17799. ISO/IEC 17799 is expected to be renamed to ISO/IEC 27002 in the future.

BS 7799, ISO 17799, and ISO/IEC 17799 have received broad international acceptance across many industries as a framework for managing information security. ISO/IEC 17799 is complementary to frameworks and standards from other organizations and is often used in conjunction with the National Institute of Standards and Technology (NIST), Special Publication 800-53 and CobIT.

From a structural perspective, ISO/IEC 17799 contains 11 security control clauses that contain 39 primary security categories and one introductory clause on risk assessment and treatment.

List 1.3 shows the eleven clauses.
1. Security Policy
2. Organizing Information Security
3. Asset Management
4. Human Resources Security
5. Physical and Environmental Security
6. Communications and Operations Management
7. Access Control
8. Information Systems Acquisition, Development, and Maintenance
9. Information Security Incident Management
10. Business Continuity Management
11. Compliance

ISO/IEC 17799 is available in PDF format from http://www.iso.org/ for CHF 200.00 (Swiss Franks).

NIST Computer Security Division Publications

Founded in 1901, NIST is an agency within the U. S. Commerce Department's Technology Administration. The mission of NIST is "to promote U.S. innovation and industrial competitiveness by advancing measurement science, standards, and technology in ways that enhance economic security and improve our quality of life." In terms of information technology security, NIST is responsible for developing standards, guidelines, and minimum information security requirements for information systems used within the U. S. Federal Government. The Computer Security Division (CSD) is the division within NIST that is tasked with developing publications that present the results of NIST studies and research on information technology security. The publications are available publicly at no cost and are issued as Drafts, Special Publications, Federal Information Processing Standards Publications (FIPS PUBS), ITL Bulletins, and Interagency Reports. The publications represent the standards, guidelines, and minimum information security requirements to deploy information systems within the U. S. Federal Government.

NIST publications have become widely adopted in the public sector by providing organizations with best practices to secure information and information systems.

List 1.4 highlights key NIST Standards and Guidelines.
- FIPS Publication 199 (Security Categorization)
- FIPS Publication 200 (Minimum Security Requirements)
- NIST Special Publication 800-18 (Security Planning)
- NIST Special Publication 800-30 (Risk Management)
- NIST Special Publication 800-37 (Certification & Accreditation)
- NIST Special Publication 800-53 (Recommended Security Controls)
- NIST Special Publication 800-53A (Security Control Assessment)
- NIST Special Publication 800-59 (National Security Systems)
- NIST Special Publication 800-60 (Security Category Mapping)

NIST publications provide a wide rage of information technology security standards and guidelines that organizations of any size can use in the development and implementation of their information security systems. The NIST publications are available at http://csrc.nist.gov/publications/index.html.

STIGS and NSA Guides

The Security Technical Implementation Guides (STIGS) and the NSA Guides are the configuration standards for the U. S. Department of Defense (DoD) Information Assurance (IA) and Information Assurance-enabled devices and systems. They are developed by the U. S. Defense Information Systems Agency (DISA) for the U. S. Department of Defense.

The IA Document Library contains STIGS that cover over 20 topics. Examples of the STIGS topics are: Active Directory, Ports and Protocols, Application Security, Database Guidance, Desktop Application Guidance, VM Guidance, and Windows 2003 Guidance.

The NSA Guides are vendor specific security configuration guides covering Applications, Database Servers, Operating Systems, Routers, Supporting Documents, Switches, VoIP and IP Telephony, Vulnerability Technical Reports, Web Servers, and Browsers and Wireless.

The STIGS and NSA Guides have become widely adopted in the public sector providing organizations with best practices to implement and secure technologies.

Chapter 1 Summary

This chapter began with a discussion about Terminal Server, followed by Terminal Server security considerations, and an introduction to Enterprise Architecture and Control Frameworks and Management Standards.

Terminal Server
- Terminal Server is the de facto Server Based Computing solution for Microsoft environments.

- Server Based Computing allows centralized management of desktops, applications, data, and network traffic.
- Terminal Server dramatically reduces bandwidth utilization over traditional computing models.
- Terminal Server reduces the amount of client software on each desktop to a single piece of client software, the RDC client.
- The RDP client is supported on Windows and Apple, Linux and UNIX.

Terminal Server Security

- Terminal Server centralizes security management of an organization's entire desktop environment, user data and network traffic.
- Server Based Computing moves the security controls from the PC desktop to centrally managed Terminal Server Desktop and the data center networks.
- Enterprise Security Architecture design principles provide a way to leverage Terminal Server to implement granular security controls.

Enterprise Architecture

- An Enterprise Architecture is an organizational wide blueprint used to achieve business objectives while maximizing the business value of information technology.
- An Enterprise Architecture consists of diagrams and a policy infrastructure.
- A policy infrastructure consists of tier 1, tier 2 and tier 3 policies.
- Tier 1 policies address broad organizational wide issues, vision and direction.
- Tier 2 policies are typically vendor agnostic that describe high level requirements.
- Tier 3 policies are vendor and procedural specific.
- Terminal Servers policies are managed in the platform architecture domain.

Control Frameworks and Management Standards

- Organizations turn to Control Frameworks and Management Standards to help develop information technology strategies that comply with regulatory mandates.
- Frameworks, standards, and guidelines provide recommendations and best practices on information security management, service management, and compliance.
- CobIT is a "framework and supporting toolset that allows managers to bridge the gap between control requirements, technical issues and business risks." (ref: ISACA)
- CobIT has become the de facto standard for auditors and Sarbanes-Oxley compliance and has been widely mapped against the "big three" standards: COSO, ITIL, and ISO 17799.
- ISO/IEC 17799 is published by the International Organization for Standardization (ISO) and the International Electrotechnical Commission (IEC) and provides guidance on security policy, staff security awareness, business continuity planning, and legal requirements.
- NIST is responsible to develop standards, guidelines, and minimum information security requirements for information systems used within the U. S. federal government.
- The Computer Security Division (CSD) is the division within NIST that is tasked with developing publications and presenting the results of NIST studies and research on information technology security.
- NIST publications are available publicly at no cost and are issued as Drafts, Special Publications, Federal Information Processing Standards Publications (FIPS PUBS), ITL Bulletins and Interagency Reports.
- The Security Technical Implementation Guides (STIGS) and the NSA Guides are the configuration standards for the U. S. Department of Defense (DoD) Information Assurance (IA) and Information Assurance-enabled devices and systems.
- The IA Document Library contains STIGS that cover over 20 topics.

Chapter 2: Terminal Server Technical Review

Chapter Overview:
This chapter provides a technical overview of Terminal Server and the interrelationships between supporting technologies that work with Terminal Server. I will also introduce infrastructure design concepts and conclude with a high level Terminal Server Reference Design. The goal of this chapter is to provide an understanding of how Terminal Server works with supporting technologies and to review infrastructure design concepts.

Understanding the evolution of information technology provides insight into the variety of technologies within our infrastructure. As we move through time, new technologies that ultimately make legacy technologies obsolete are developed and brought to market. Mainframes are a good example of a legacy technology that was threatened by new technologies; however, history has proven that Mainframe technology was not replaced by newer technologies. Another example is Java and Web applications, which promised to obsolete the client-server model. Both Java and Web applications have gained broad acceptance, but they have not replaced the client-server model. In contrast to the market hype, organizations adopt new technologies with the hope to replace older ones; but after a short period of time, they learn that most new technologies do not replace the older ones. They inevitably end up supporting new technologies along side older ones, which adds to their technology portfolio and introduces complexity and security challenges.

The Server Based Computing model is based on centralization of computing resources similar to the Mainframe model. A Mainframe is a large, central computer with a lot of memory, storage capacity, and fast processors that runs a specialized operating system to handle all the processing for large operations or tasks. The primary difference between Mainframe computing and Server Based Computing is that Mainframes are large central computers that run specialized Mainframe hardware and applications, whereas today's Server Based Computing solutions are smaller PC-based systems that operate on inexpensive commodity hardware and run off-the-shelf desktop applications. Server Based Computing requires the use of a multi-user operating system, such as Windows, Linux, or UNIX. A multi-user operating system allows multiple users to share the same computer at the same time and/or different times.

Figure 2.1 shows the Server Based Computing model with a dumb terminal accessing a Terminal Server. The RDP client displays the Terminal Server desktop on the screen of the dumb terminal.

Figure 2.1

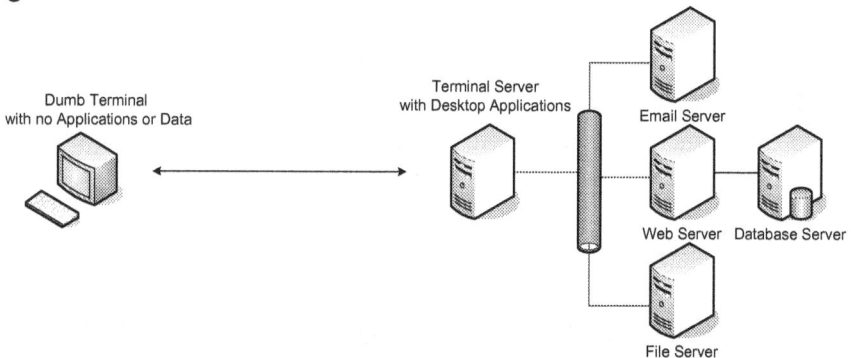

Today Microsoft has implemented a Session Manager layer in their desktop and server platforms allowing multiple, concurrent users to run separate and isolated sessions. Hardware resources permitting, a single Terminal Server could simultaneously host hundreds of isolated user sessions. Terminal Server separates an application's logic from its user interface (UI), allowing an application to run on a Terminal Server and to be displayed on the screen of a terminal. Only keystrokes, mouse clicks, screen updates, and print jobs travel between the server and Terminal Server client. Therefore, application performance does not depend on local computing resources or bandwidth limitations as is the case with client-server, Java or Web applications.

With Terminal Server, all of the application and data processing is executed on the Terminal Server, hence, the term "Server Based Computing." Applications are installed, managed, and executed on the Terminal Server, and only keystrokes, mouse clicks and screen updates traverse the network between the server and client using the remote desktop protocol (RDP). Users interact with applications and data from a Terminal Server desktop that looks identical to a Windows PC desktop.

Because applications are completely executed on the server, very little computing resources are required on the terminal, be it a PC or thin client. A thin client is a network device with an embedded operating system requiring no hard drive, minimal processing, and memory resources. Thin clients come with rich feature sets similar to PCs, allowing them to work in any Terminal Server environment at a fraction of the cost of a PC.

An RDP client is a software application that establishes and maintains a connection between a terminal and a Terminal Server. Today RDP clients are typically referred to as RDC, which stands for Remote Desktop Client. RDC is the default Windows XP Terminal Server client. There are many publicly available RDP clients supporting Windows, MAC, Linux, and UNIX operating systems.

The acronym RDP stands for Remote Desktop Protocol, which is Microsoft's remote networking protocol used exclusively by Terminal Server. The RDP protocol is a multiple-channel remote networking protocol that was originally developed in the mid 1990s. RDP allows for separate virtual channels to carry device communications, such as mouse, keyboard, sound, printer and screen data between an RDP client and a Terminal Server. In terms of security, this architecture provides the ability to turn on or off virtual channels via Group Policy in order to meet specific security requirement. For example, local drive mapping is a virtual channel that allows a Terminal Server to map a client's local hard drives. When local drive mapping is enabled, users can access data on their local hard drive or CDROM from a Terminal Server session. Local drive mapping can introduce risk because data can traverse from a compromised workstation to a Terminal Server. The ability to disable virtual channels is a security benefit allowing organizations to meet a wide variety of security and regulatory requirements.

The virtual channel settings can be configured locally on a Terminal Server by using the Terminal Services Configuration utility (tscc.msc) or centrally via Active Directory. Group Policy can be configured in Active Directory by editing the desired Group Policy Object in the following location:
Computer Configurations > Administrative Templates > Windows Components > Terminal Services > Client/Server data redirection.

Table 2.1 lists key security related virtual channel Group Policy settings.

Table 2.1

Virtual Channel Setting	Explanation
Do not allow clipboard redirection	Determines whether to disable sharing of clipboard (cut and paste) contents between Terminal Server applications and a local applications during a Terminal Server session.
Allow audio redirection	By default Terminal Server on Windows Server 2003 disables audio redirection.
Do not allow COM port redirection	Determines whether to disable the mapping of client COM ports during a Terminal Server session.
Do not allow client printer redirection	Determines whether to disable mapping of client printers during a Terminal Server session.
Do not allow LPT port redirection	Determines whether to disable the redirection of data to client LPT ports during a Terminal Server session.
Do not allow driver redirection	Determines whether to disable the mapping of client drives during a Terminal Server session.

RDP functions as a virtual display, keyboard, and mouse on the server. Instead of sending video output to the VGA port, Terminal Services redirect it to the video channel in the RDP stack. Doing so transmits the display information across the network and draws it on the client's workstation screen. RDP also takes keystrokes and mouse movements at the remote client and transmits them back to the Terminal Server, where they are processed as if they came from a local keyboard and mouse. By default RDP traffic runs over port 3389 using TCP.

Figure 2.2 shows the interaction between an RDP client and a Terminal Server.

Figure 2.2

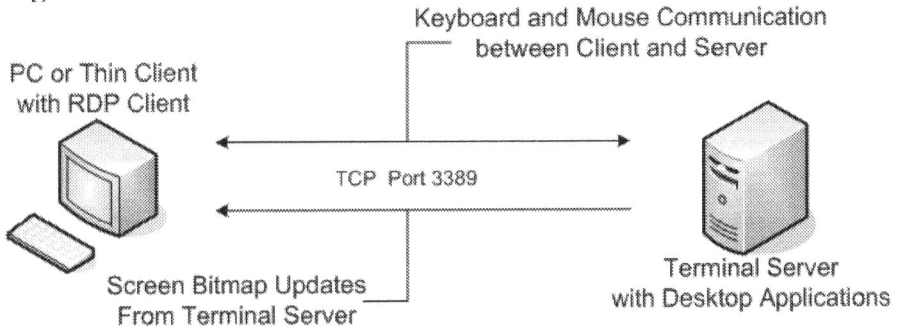

RDP traffic is minimal as only keyboard, mouse, screen updates, and occasional print traffic travel over the wire. Server Based Computing actually centralizes network traffic as the bulk of traffic flows between back-end systems, such as between Terminal Servers and email, web, database and file servers on the same or adjacent network. From a design perspective, Terminal Servers should be placed next to the data. Placing the Terminal Servers next to the data ensures that as little data as possible traverses over a network, thereby promoting efficiencies in bandwidth management and bandwidth utilization and providing a positive and consistent user experience.

Figure 2.3 shows the placement of a Terminal Server, other back-end systems, and an RDP client.

Figure 2.3

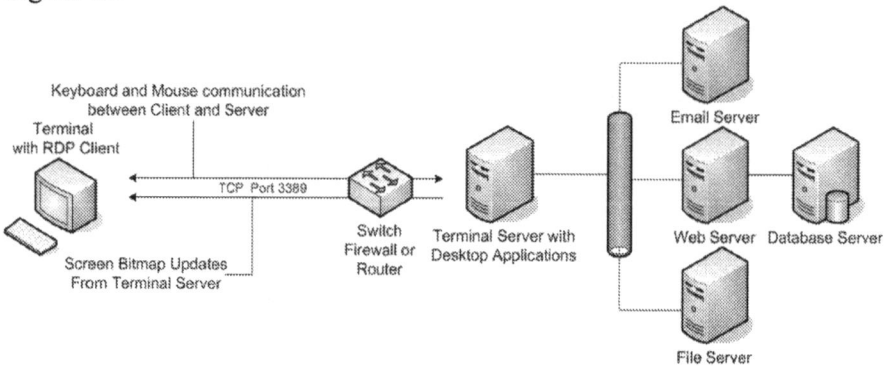

By default RDP traffic can be configured to use one of four levels of encryption. Terminal Server on Windows Server 2003 supports Low, Client Compatible, Federal Information Processing Standard (FIPS) Compliant, and High encryption levels. Encryption levels can be locally or centrally configured via Group Policy. The encryption algorithm used depends on the configured encryption mode. For example, not all RDP clients can support FIPS Compliant and High encryption levels, so in a mixed environment with legacy and non-Windows clients, Medium encryption may be the highest supported encryption level. The RDP protocol uses Triple DES (3DES) and Secure Hash Algorithm v1.0 (SHA1) for FIPS compliant connections or RC4 symmetric encryption algorithm with an MD5 hash with Low, Client Compatible, and High encryption levels.

List 2.1 shows each encryption level.
- FIPS: encrypts both the data sent from client to server and the data sent from server to client by using the Federal Information Processing Standard (FIPS) encryption algorithms with Microsoft cryptographic modules. This feature is supported on Windows 2000 or Windows XP with the RDP 5.2 client.
- High: encrypts both the data sent from client to server and the data sent from server to client using a 128-bit key. Legacy RDP clients that do not support this level of encryption will not be able to connect.
- Medium: encrypts both the data sent from client to server and the data sent from server to client, by using a 56-bit key if the client is a Windows 2000 or above, or a 40-bit key if the client

is an earlier version. This level is ideal when Terminal Servers are supporting mixed or legacy clients.

- Low: encrypts only the data sent from client to server, using either a 56-bit or 40-bit key, depending on the client version. The data sent from the server to the client is not encrypted.

The encryption levels can be configured locally on a Terminal Server using the Terminal Services Configuration utility (tscc.msc) or centrally via Active Directory. The Group Policies can be configured in Active Directory by editing the desired Group Policy Object from the following location:
Computer Configurations > Administrative Templates > Windows Components > Terminal Services > Encryption and Security.

Figure 2.4 shows the Group Policy "Set client connection encryption level Properties."

Figure 2.4

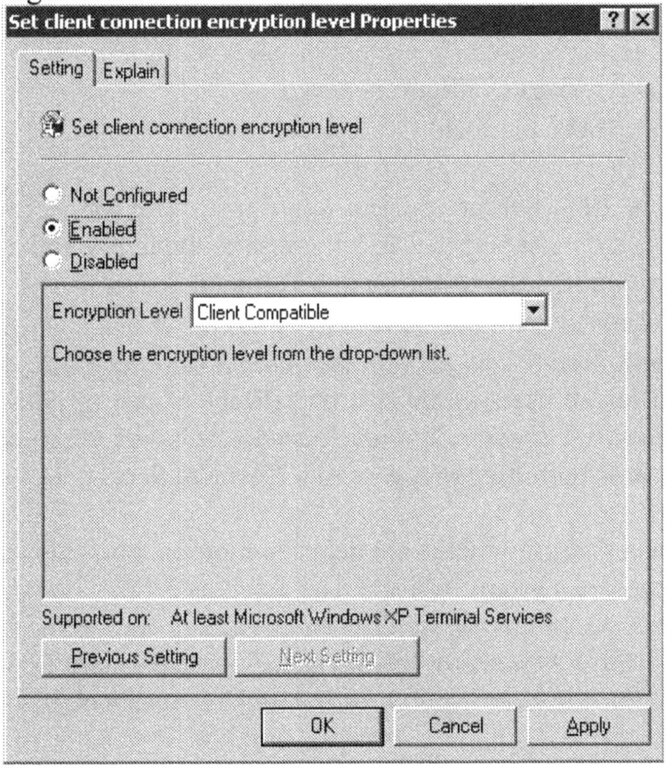

Terminal Server Access Requirements

Windows Server 2003 has three different layers of access rights that control who can log on to a Terminal Server. To allow users to log on to a Terminal Server, the following settings must be made:

- The *Allow logon through Terminal Services* right:
  - Windows 2000 required the *log on locally* right to all users to gain access to a Terminal Server. The *log on locally* right allows users to log on at the console of the server, bypassing RDP level restrictions. This configuration gave users unnecessary privileges and was once considered a material weakness.
  - Windows 2003 Server fixed the problem by separating the right to log on to the console from the right to log on through Terminal Services. By default, the *Allow logon through Terminal Services* right is granted to Administrators and to the Remote Desktop Users group.
- Permission to use RDP:
  - Administrators can configure permissions on RDP with the Terminal Services Configuration tool.
  - Windows 2000, the local Users group, is granted access to RDP.
  - Windows 2003 Server restricts this right to the local Remote Desktop Users group. Users must be explicitly added to this group in order to log on to a Terminal Server.
- The *Allow logon to terminal server* check box:
  - By default, the *Allow logon to terminal server* check box is enabled for all users in their Active Directory user properties. The *Allow logon to terminal server* check box controls if the user is permitted to log on to a Terminal Server.

Two of the three access requirements are dependent on membership in the Remote Desktop Users group. When a user receives a "You do not have permission to access this session" error message, one of these three settings (*The Allow logon through Terminal Services* right, Permission to use RDP or the *Allow logon to terminal server* check box) is the problem.

Application Access

The default behavior with Terminal Server is to assume that all legitimate users have access to all applications installed on a Terminal Server. The default behavior is widely adopted and used in most deployments because of its simplicity. To meet business and regulatory requirements, many organizations implement application access restrictions to control which applications are available to specific users. There are two strategies used to employ application restrictions: black-list or white-list policies. A black-list policy is used when an administrator explicitly specifies which applications are not allowed to execute, and all other applications are allowed. A white-list policy is used when an administrator explicitly specifies which applications are allowed to execute, and nothing else is allowed.

Application Access Restrictions

Application access restrictions are typically implemented to meet business objectives and regulatory mandates. For example, access to financial applications may need to be restricted to a specific user or group of users in order to comply with the Sarbanes-Oxley Act. Another example would be the need to restrict access to a payroll application from the general user population. A wide variety of integrated solutions are on the Windows Server platform to apply application access restrictions. One strategy is to leverage the default behavior so that all users can execute the majority of installed applications excluding specific applications with access restrictions; this procedure follows the black-list model. Another strategy is to use the white-list model to specify which applications are allowed to execute and nothing else is allowed. Implementing Terminal Server silos is another strategy in which only specific users are granted access to a dedicated Terminal Server silo that hosts restricted applications. Many applications require a secondary authentication, which is an application level access restriction as well.

The next sections will introduce five application access restriction options: NTFS file system level restrictions, Software Restriction policies, the Run only allowed Windows Applications Group Policy, Terminal Server Silos, and application level access restrictions.

Note: The implementation of Application Access Restrictions requires extensive testing to ensure that applications function properly and that the user environment is not too restrictive. Each organization should evaluate its unique requirements to develop Application Access Restrictions that provide sufficient security and manageability, without limiting user productivity.

NTFS File System Restrictions

NTFS file system restrictions can be employed to restrict access to an application's executable to approved users or groups. NTFS file system restrictions follows the black-list model where administrators explicitly specify what applications are not allowed to execute, and all other applications are allowed. This method of enforcing application restrictions is widely adopted and typically used together with the default behavior. The use of NTFS file system restrictions with the default behavior allows a single server farm to host an organization's entire application portfolio without the need to dedicate servers to host restricted access applications.

Configuring NTFS file system application restrictions is identical to the configuration of NTFS file and directory security. In a Windows Server 2003 environment, NTFS file system permissions can be configured centrally using Active Directory and Group Policy. Centralized configuration of NTFS file system application restrictions with Active Directory and Group Policy allows an organization to centralize the configuration, enforcement, and auditing of NTFS file system level application restrictions.

When properly implemented, NTFS file level security is very difficult to circumvent. Regardless of how users access the server, restricted applications will only execute for users with the appropriate NTFS rights.

Software Restriction Policies & Run Only Allowed Windows Applications Group Policy

Software Restriction Policies were introduced with Windows XP and Windows 2003 Server and have effectively replaced the Windows

2000 Run Only Allowed Windows Applications Group Policy. Microsoft Software Restriction Policies provides the integrated framework to implement granular application execution policies by using Active Directory Group Policy without the need of any additional 3rd party software. Software Restriction Policies are supported on Windows XP and the Windows Server 2003 platform.

Software Restriction Policies provide the security controls to restrict application and file access execution and to mitigate the introduction of hostile code through email or web browsing, such as script based viruses or Active X controls. This method is more restrictive and secure than Terminal Server's default behavior and provides more granular control over application execution than NTFS file system restrictions.

Terminal Server Silos

Another strategy is to implement a siloed environment as described in Chapter 1. One Terminal Server silo is used to support the general user population leveraging the default behavior, and dedicated Terminal Server silos are established to host restricted access applications. Terminal Server silos allow the appropriate security controls, such as auditing and encryption, to be implemented based on the sensitivity of the data or application hosted on a silo. This strategy is widely adopted and is typically used with software restriction policies in order to satisfy regulatory mandates.

Application Level Restrictions

Application level restriction requires users to enter secondary credentials, such as user name and passwords, to gain access to an application. Applications that employ application level restrictions typically maintain their own user database, which is not integrated or synchronized with Active Directory. Typically this approach leads to password policy violations because users write down their secondary user credentials on a piece of paper or on some pad near their computer.

In many cases, application level restrictions require a Single Sign-on solution in order to meet business or regulatory objectives. A Single

Sign-on solution will securely store and automatically submit user credentials to applications that employ application level restrictions.

Application Access Conclusion

Terminal Server provides tremendous flexibility in terms of centralized application deployment and granular application access entitlements. Organizations can use a single Terminal Server farm to host their entire application portfolio by using a black-list model and leveraging the default behavior with NTFS file system restrictions. If a more restrictive and secure environment is required, a white-list model can be implemented using Active Directory Group Policy, application level restrictions, and silos. These application access options allow organizations to meet business and regulatory requirements using proven industry standards.

Terminal Services Technologies

This section will look at the technologies behind Terminal Server. We will review Terminal Services, Session Directory, Terminal Server license server, and a Terminal Server farm.

Terminal Services and the Session Manager

Terminal Services, a Windows service, enables multi-user technology by implementing a Session Manager layer between the system and user layers. The Session Manager replies to new session requests by creating a separate instance of the Win32 subsystem, WIN32K.SYS, for each user session. The Session Manager then executes the client-server runtime subsystem, CRSS.EXE, and the Windows logon service, WINLOGON.EXE, within the session.

Figure 2.5 shows which processes make up Terminal Services divided between user mode and kernel mode and indicates whether they are per server or per session.

Figure 2.5

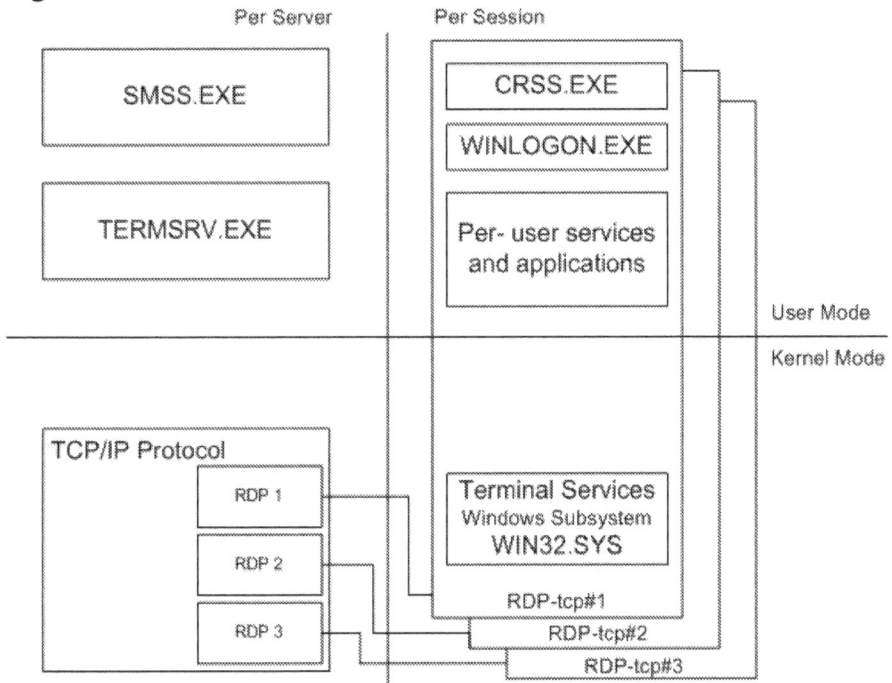

Figure 2.5 illustrates the process that allows multiple user sessions to run simultaneously on today's Windows operating systems. The Session Manager directs users to their sessions and then directs the applications, services, and resources to the new session. Session Manager assigns each session a unique ID and address space so that resource and network requests can be directed to the correct user.

Session Directory

The Session Directory service is a Windows Server 2003 Enterprise Edition feature that provides a single point of entry into a load-balanced Terminal Server farm. The Session Directory service is installed by default on all editions of Windows Server 2003. It is used in conjunction with a load-balancing solution like Microsoft's load-balancing service or a third-party hardware load-balancer. Session Directory acts as a RDP session load-balancer, connecting users to the least busy server while maintaining a jet database of active sessions within the Terminal Server farm. This feature enables disconnected users to reconnect to their active, disconnected session at the same

SECURING MICROSOFT TERMINAL SERVICES

server. When a user connects to a server farm through the Session Directory server, the Session Directory checks the list of active and disconnected sessions. If the username is found in the database, the connection is directed to the server running the session.

Windows Server 2003, Standard Edition, may be used to run the Session Directory service, although all servers in the Terminal Server farm must be on Windows Server 2003 Enterprise Edition to take advantage of Session Directory functionality.

List 2.1 explains how the Session Directory works.
1. An incoming connection to the server farm is load-balanced to a Terminal Server, which presents a logon prompt.
2. When the user authenticates, the Terminal Server that received the original client logon request sends the username to the Session Directory server.
3. The Session Directory server checks the username in the database and sends the result to the requesting Terminal Server.
   a. If the user has no disconnected sessions, the logon process continues from the server that received the initial connection.
   b. If the user has a disconnected session, the Terminal Server that received the original client logon request sends the client information to the server hosting the disconnected session, and the user authenticates on the server hosting the disconnected session.
4. Once the user accesses the disconnected session, the Session Directory is updated.

A load-balanced farm is accessed by end users with a single virtual IP address (VIP). A virtual IP address is shared among multiple computers and is typically used for load balancing. Intra machine communication, such as Terminal Server to Session Directory server, is RPC on port 135 and on randomly allocated high TCP ports. The name of the system service for the Session Directory is "tssdis".

To use the Session Directory, the following three configurations are needed:

1. Turn on the Session Directory service. (Session Directory Server)
2. Add each Terminal Server domain account to the Session Directory Computers group. (Session Directory Server)
3. Configure each Windows Server 2003 Enterprise Edition Terminal Server in the farm to participate in the Session Directory. (Terminal Servers)

The first time the Session Directory service is started, a new local group is created on the host called Session Directory Computers. By default, the Session Directory Computers group is empty. Access to Session Directory functionality must be explicitly granted by adding each Terminal Server's domain computer account to the Session Directory group. The Session Directory service will only accept connections from servers in the Session Directory local group. The accounts can be added individually or by creating a domain group containing the Terminal Servers and then adding the domain group to the Session Directory group.

Note: The Session Directory may not work with non-Windows clients in a load-balanced environment. The Session Directory uses a token to pass information to the load balancer and RDP client. If the load-balancing solution or non-Windows clients do not support tokens, reconnection to disconnected sessions will not work.

From a security perspective, it is important to consider what happens when the Session Directory fails. Other than losing Session Directory functionality, logon times will increase as each Terminal Server attempts to connect to the Session Directory server, which could affect the availability of the Terminal Server farm. The Session Directory service supports Microsoft's clustering technology, which should be considered to provide fault tolerance and high-availability.

Terminal Services Licensing
For a Terminal Server to accept connections after the 120-day trial period, a terminal services licensing server must be configured. To connect to a Windows Server 2003 Terminal Server, clients need to be issued a Windows Server 2003 license token, which is referred to as a CAL (Client Access License). Windows Server 2003 CALs can only

be issued by a Windows Server 2003 terminal services license server. A Windows 2000 services license server cannot issue Windows Server 2003 CALs. Terminal services licensing consists of the Microsoft Clearinghouse, one or more Windows Server 2003 terminal services licensing servers (any edition of Windows Server 2003), and Terminal Servers. From a Terminal Server console, the Microsoft Clearinghouse can be accessed to activate license servers and to acquire and install license key packs on the terminal services licensing server. The Microsoft Clearinghouse is accessible via the Internet, through a web page, or by telephone.

Terminal services licensing servers store all terminal services tokens while continually monitoring all tokens that have been issued to computers or users. Terminal Servers must be able to communicate with a terminal services licensing server in order to issue permanent tokens. Intra machine communication, such as Terminal Server to terminal services licensing server communication, is RPC on port 135 and randomly allocated high TCP ports. The name of the system service for terminal services licensing is "TermServLicensing".

Note: Inactivated license servers can only issue temporary licenses.

Terminal services licensing can be installed on domain controllers or member servers in Enterprise license server or domain license server mode. The primary difference between the two modes is the license server discovery process. Domain controllers or member servers configured in Enterprise license server mode are automatically discovered by Terminal Servers; license servers that are configured in domain license server mode are not automatically discovered. Terminal Servers cache the names of discovered license servers in the following locations of the registry:
HKEY_LOCAL_MACHINE\Software\Microsoft\MSLicensing\Param eters\EnterpriseServerMulti (Enterprise license servers)
HKEY_LOCAL_MACHINE\Software\Microsoft\MSLicensing\Param eters\DomainLicenseServerMulti (Domain license servers)

If the discovery process fails, and no license server is found, a Terminal Server will automatically run a discovery once every hour. After a license server is found, no additional discoveries are made until all of the cached license servers in the registry are unavailable.

34

Environments with a member server in domain license server mode need to configure each Terminal Server with a preferred license server. Configuring a preferred license server requires a registry modification by adding a subkey with the hostname of the preferred license server on each Terminal Server in HKEY_LOCAL_MACHINE\SYSTEM \CurrentControlSet\Services\TermService\Parameters\LicenseServers subkey.

From a security perspective, it is important to consider high availability when designing a Terminal services licensing solution. When Terminal services licensing fails, the availability of the system is at risk because users could be denied access. Microsoft's recommended configuration for license server high availability is to install a minimum of two license servers with Terminal Services CALs. Each license server should have 50% of the CALs, effectively load balancing the licenses between license servers providing high availability.

Terminal Server Farm
When multiple Terminal Servers are load-balanced, it is commonly referred to as a Terminal Server farm. A Terminal Server farm consists of a network load-balancing solution, two or more Terminal Servers, and optionally a Session Directory server. A load-balanced farm is accessed by end users with a single virtual IP address; therefore, each Terminal Server in a farm should be identically provisioned and configured to ensure consistency.

A Terminal Server farm allows organizations to scale out their Terminal Server environment by adding machines to the farm to increase capacity. A Terminal Server farm can be load-balanced with Microsoft's integrated load-balancing service or a third-party hardware load-balancer.

Figure 2.6 shows an example Terminal Server farm.

Figure 2.6

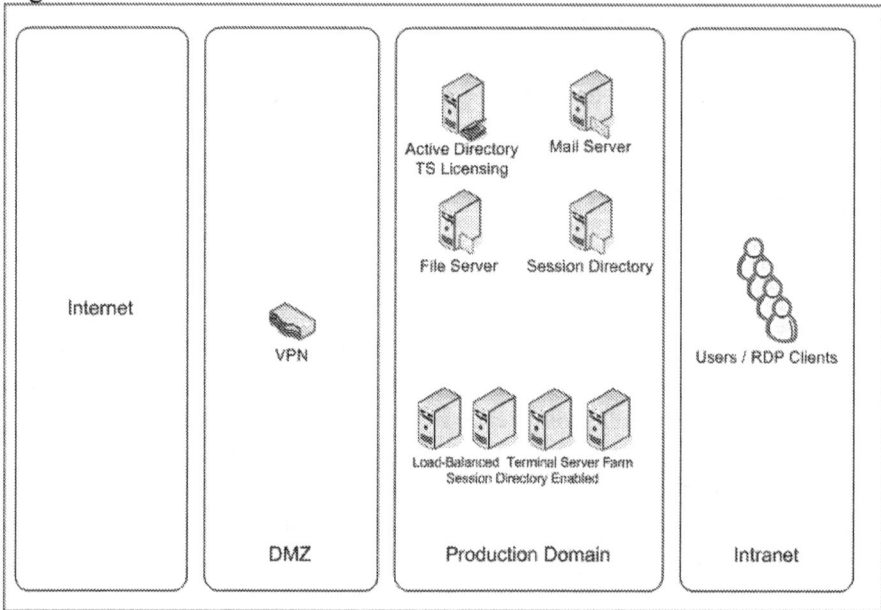

From a security perspective, it is important to consider fault tolerance and high availability when designing a Terminal Server farm. Fault tolerance and high availability for Terminal Server licensing, Session Directory, and Load-Balancing should be considered to ensure the availability of the system.

Figure 2.7 shows a Terminal Server farm configured for high availability with two license servers. Each license server has 50% of the CALs, a Session Directory cluster, and Microsoft's Load-Balancing Services.

Figure 2.7

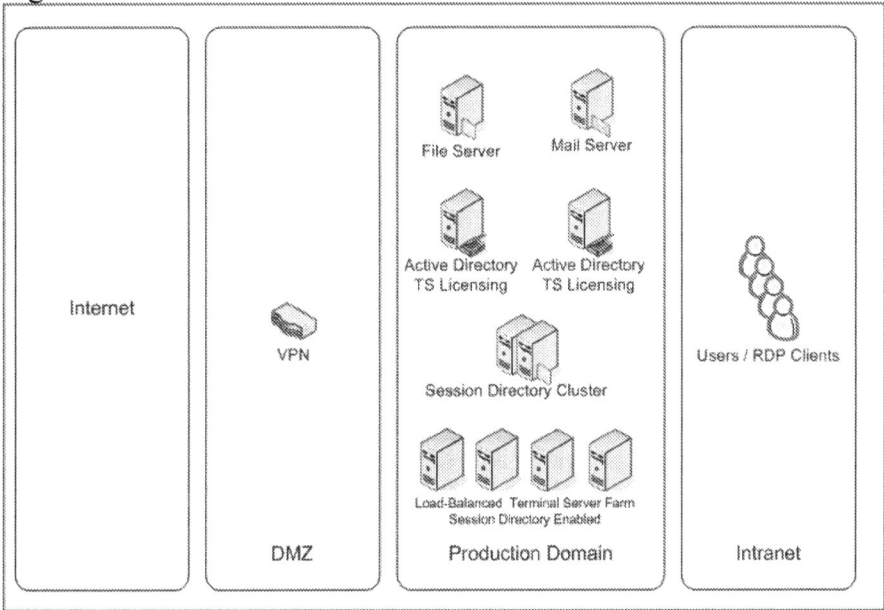

Terminal Server Reference Design

The Terminal Server Reference Design presented in this section is a high level baseline that represents a secure, flexible, and scaleable framework. It contains software, hardware, and storage components that enable an organization to centralize the deployment and management of its Windows desktop and Windows applications infrastructure using Microsoft Terminal Server.

Figure 2.8 shows an architectural overview of the Terminal Server Reference Design. Please note that each security domain (i.e. uncontrolled, controlled, restricted, and intranet) is a separate network segment. A firewall and/or a router are used to filter network traffic between security domains.

Figure 2.8

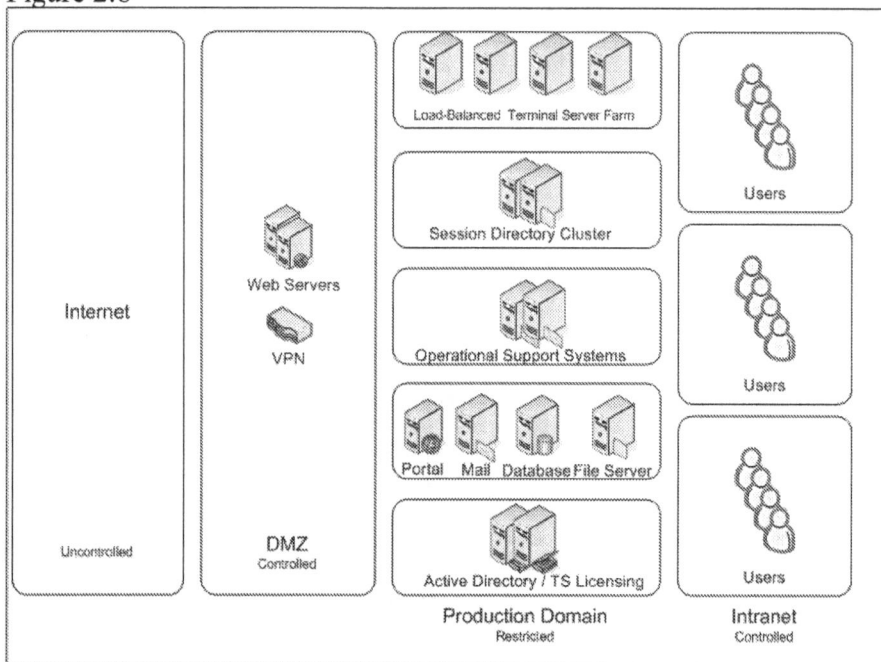

As shown in Figure 2.8, there are multiple components within the Terminal Server Reference Design. These components include, but are not limited to, the following:

1. The Terminal Server Farm.
2. Required Terminal Server Infrastructure Services.
3. Required Microsoft Infrastructure Services.
4. Back-end Application and Data Storage Servers.
5. Required Network Infrastructure.
6. Operational Support Systems (OSS) includes help desk, system and SLA monitoring, and capacity planning as well as application, service pack, and hotfix provisioning.

In addition to the components listed above, there are at least four distinct network subnets along with additional isolated subnets within the restricted security domain. These network subnets include the

1. Uncontrolled
2. Controlled
3. Restricted
4. Intranet

Note: See Chapter 5 for a detailed explanation about the network topology in Figure 2.8.

Users access the system from either the Internet or within the LAN environment. From the Internet, users are routed to one of the Terminal Server farm servers via a VPN. From the LAN, users are routed to one of the Terminal Server farm servers via a router. Depending on the type of application and data request, a connection to a back-end application server and a back-end data store may also have to be made to deliver an application or data.

The Terminal Server Farm

Multiple Terminal Servers that are load-balanced are commonly referred to as a Terminal Server farm. A Terminal Server farm consists of a network load-balancing solution, two or more Terminal Servers, and optionally a Session Directory server. A load-balanced farm is accessed by end users with a single virtual IP address; therefore, each Terminal Server in a farm should be identically provisioned and configured to ensure consistency.

A Terminal Server farm allows organizations to scale out their Terminal Server environment by adding machines to the farm to increase capacity by providing robust, centralized application delivery and management capability. It is scalable, reliable, manageable, and secure. And it offers predictability in terms of performance, user experience and cost.

Required Terminal Server Infrastructure Services

A Terminal Server farm consists of a network load-balancing solution, two or more Terminal Servers, and an optional Session Directory server and a licensing server.

Load-Balancing

A Terminal Server farm can be load-balanced with Microsoft's integrated load-balancing service or a third-party hardware load balancer.

Load Balancers allows a group of servers to be configured as a load-balanced cluster with a single Virtual IP address (VIP). Users access the cluster with the DNS name associated with the Virtual IP address.

Session Directory
The Session Directory service is an optional feature that provides a single point of entry into a load-balanced Terminal Server farm. The Session Directory service is used together with a load-balancing solution. Session Directory acts as a RDP session load-balancer, connecting users to the least busy server while maintaining a database of active sessions within the Terminal Server farm. This feature enables disconnected users to reconnect to their active, disconnected session on the same server.

Terminal Services Licensing
Terminal services licensing consists of the Microsoft Clearinghouse, one or more Windows Server 2003 terminal services licensing servers (any edition of Windows Server 2003), and Terminal Servers.

From a security perspective, it is important to consider high availability when designing a Terminal Server farm, fault tolerance, and high availability for Terminal Server licensing; Session Directory and Load-Balancing must be considered in order to ensure the availability of the system while meeting regulatory mandates.

Required Microsoft Network Infrastructure Services
The Microsoft Network Infrastructure Services required to support a Terminal Server farm includes Active Directory, DNS and File Services.

Back-End Application and Data Storage Servers
Many applications require a back-end application and/or data storage. An example of this is an N-tier web application. The front end resides on a web server, and the data resides on a SQL Server database.

Required Network Infrastructure Services
The required network infrastructure services required to support a Terminal Server farm include firewalls, VPNs, switches, routers and load balancers.

Operational Support Systems (OSS)
Operational Support Systems (OSS) encompasses technologies, services, and solutions that help an organization efficiently manage their environment and provide support to their users.

Chapter 2 Summary
This chapter provided a technical overview of Terminal Server and the inter-relationships between supporting technologies that work together with Terminal Server.

Terminal Server technical review
- RDP is an application layer multiple-channel remote networking protocol that functions as a virtual display, keyboard and mouse on the server.
- An RDP client is a software application that establishes and maintains a connection between a terminal with an RDP client and a Terminal Server.
- Terminal Server in Windows Server 2003 has three different layers of access rights. Two of the three access rights requirements are dependent on membership in the Remote Desktop Users group.
- The default behavior with Terminal Server is to assume that all users have access to all applications installed on a Terminal Server.
- Application access restrictions are sometimes necessary to meet business objectives and regulatory mandates.
- Application access can be controlled using file level rights, Software Restriction policies, the Run Only Allowed Windows Applications Group Policy, or 3rd party solutions.

Terminal Services and the Session Manager
- A Windows service enables multi-user technology by implementing a Session Manager layer between the system and user layers.
- The Session Manager replies to new session requests by creating a separate instance of the Win32 subsystem, WIN32K.SYS, for each user session.

- The Session Manager directs users to their sessions and then directs the applications, services, and resources to the new session.
- The Session Manager assigns each session a unique ID and address space so that resource and network requests can be directed to the correct user.

Session Directory

- The Session Directory service is a Windows Server 2003 Enterprise Edition feature that provides a single point of entry into a load-balanced Terminal Server farm.
- The Session Directory service is installed by default on all editions of Windows Server 2003.
- Session Directory service is used in conjunction with a load-balancing solution and acts as a RDP session load-balancer by connecting users to the least busy server while maintaining a database of active sessions within the Terminal Server farm.
- Terminal Server to Session Directory server communication is RPC TCP traffic on port 135 and on randomly allocated high TCP ports.
- The first time the Session Directory service is started, a new local group is created on the host called Session Directory Computers, which by default is empty.
- Access to Session Directory functionality must be explicitly granted by adding each Terminal Server's domain computer account to the Session Directory group.
- When the Session Directory fails, other than losing Session Directory functionality, logon times will increase.
- The Session Directory service supports Microsoft's clustering, which should be considered to provide fault tolerance and high availability.

Terminal Services Licensing

- For a Terminal Server to accept connections after the 120-day trial period, a terminal services licensing server must be configured.

- Terminal services licensing consists of the Microsoft Clearinghouse, one or more Windows Server 2003 terminal services licensing servers, and Terminal Servers.
- Terminal services licensing servers store all terminal services tokens while continually monitoring all tokens that have been issued to computers or users.
- Intra machine communication, such as Terminal Server to terminal services, to licensing server communication, is RPC TCP traffic on port 135 and randomly allocated high TCP ports.
- The name of the system service for terminal services licensing is "TermServLicensing".
- Microsoft's recommended configuration for license server high availability is to install a minimum of two license servers with Terminal Services CALs.

Terminal Server Farm
- Multiple load-balanced Terminal Servers are commonly referred to as a Terminal Server farm.
- A Terminal Server farm consists of a network load-balancing solution, two or more Terminal Servers, and optionally a Session Directory server.
- A load-balanced farm is accessed by end users with a single virtual IP address.
- It is important to consider high availability when designing a Terminal Server farm; fault tolerance and high availability for Terminal Server licensing, Session Directory and Load Balancing.

Chapter 3: Terminal Server and Supporting Computing Models

Chapter Overview:
This chapter will review how Server Based Computing complements and improves the performance and security of a wide variety of computing models including client-server, N-tier, Traditional Networking, and Mainframe computing. Performance and security are improved with each computing model by using the same principle, moving the client software from PCs to centrally managed Terminal Servers.

Client-server & N-tier Models
Client-server and N-tier computing models distribute application processing, data, and network traffic between PCs and servers. The Client-server Computing Model has been in use since the late 1980s and has been widely adopted in the public and private sectors. It distributes the processing of applications among different servers in the network. In this model, there is a client workstation, usually a PC, and front- and back-end servers (in most cases, the back-end server hosts a database). The client makes a request to the front-end server, and the front-end server acts as an intermediary between the client and the back-end server. The front-end server passes the query to the back-end server, and then the back-end server retrieves the requested information, formats it, and sends it back to the client. Note that the distinction between client-server and N-tier is that client-server refers to older multiple tier applications like email and N-tier refers to multiple tier web applications.

In a client-server environment, client-server software is installed and maintained on the PC and local computing resources such as processor, memory, and disk are used to run the client-server software. The application and data processing is done on the PC; back-end processing is done on the respective back-end server. PCs communicate directly to the respective back-end server. Application data can be stored locally on a PC as well as on servers. All traffic between PCs and servers travel over the network. The client-server model is most prevalent in today's business environments.

Figure 3.1 shows PCs in a typical client-server environment with client-server software communicating over the network to their respective back-end server.

Figure 3.1

PCs Hosting
Applications and Data

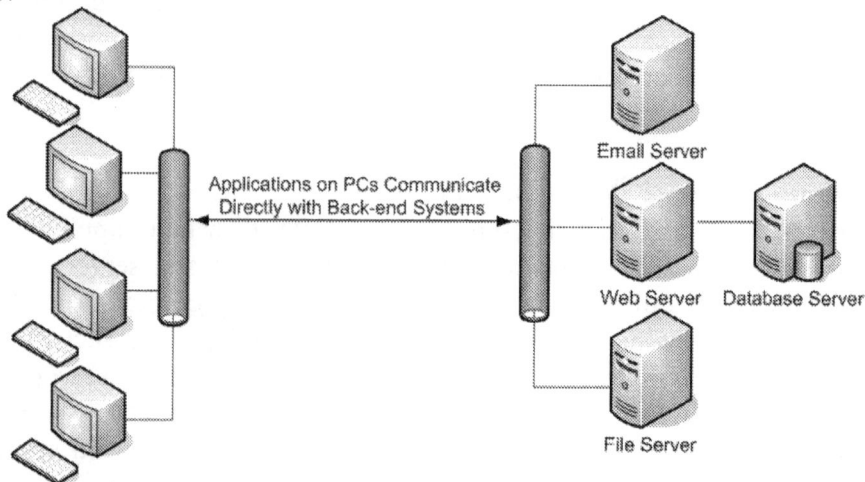

Applications on PCs Communicate
Directly with Back-end Systems

Email Server

Web Server   Database Server

File Server

To better explain the difference between client-server and the Server Based Computing, let's review the client-server communication between an email client and email server. Email is a common client-server solution that has a centralized mail server within a distributed client environment. The email client software is distributed, installed, and configured on each PC. Each PC then communicates directly with a mail server using one or more services, protocols, and ports, depending on business requirements.

Table 3.1 shows the service, protocol, and port used for email client to server communication.

Table 3.1

Service	Transport Protocol	Port
POP3	TCP	110
IMAP	TCP	143
SMTP	TCP	25
HTTP	TCP	80
HTTPS	TCP	443

Email client to server communication can rely on one or more services and protocols for client to server communication. Email bandwidth utilization with any of the listed services is considered moderate to heavy depending on a variety of factors, such as email content, attachment size, and client to server synchronization schedules.

Figure 3.2 shows email client to mail server traffic.

Figure 3.2

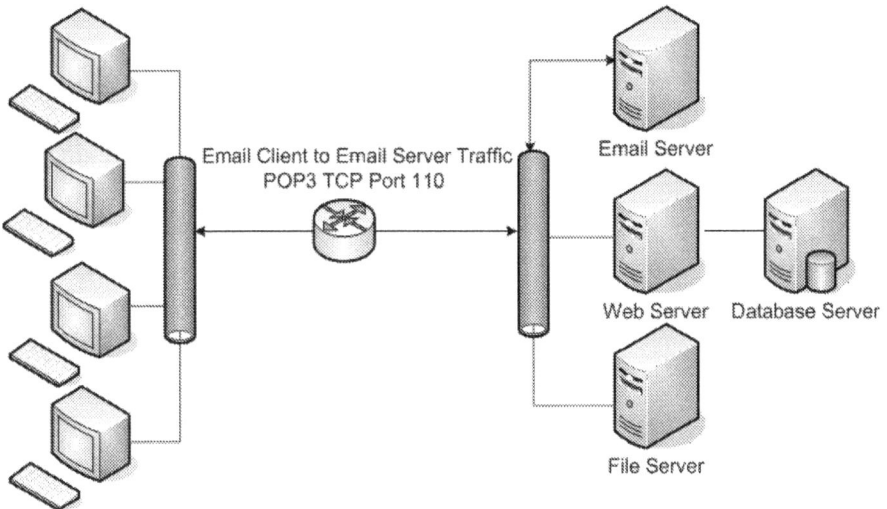

PCs with Email Client

Email Client to Email Server Traffic
POP3 TCP Port 110

Email Server

Web Server   Database Server

File Server

Figure 3.2 shows four PCs with locally installed email clients, with each client communicating directly to an email server. The router is filtering traffic, allowing POP3 traffic to flow from each PC to the Email Server.

Server Based Computing with Terminal Server compliments and improves client-server computing by moving the client software from the PCs to centrally managed Terminal Servers. Server Based Computing centralizes the administration and management of client-server applications along with the centralization and management of network traffic.

Because desktop applications are centrally managed in the data center on Terminal Servers, updates and patches management are greatly simplified in contrast to a client-server model where applications are managed on each PC. Terminal Server eliminates the risk of updating PCs that may be off-line or PCs with faulty software distribution clients or users who simply refuse to run updates. Additionally, because all applications are executing on the Terminal Servers, no information is cached locally on the PCs, thereby reducing the risk of proprietary information residing in a non-secured PC. The applications deployed in a Terminal Server environment minimize the need for open ports between the user and data center networks, thereby eliminating multiple entry points for attackers and malware into the network. Terminal Server uses one port for client-server communication. Traditional client-server applications require a variety of ports as shown above in Figure 3.1. Maintaining a small list of ports for all client-server access greatly simplifies the management and security of the data center network.

In contrast to client-server traffic, which is considered moderate to heavy, RDP traffic is minimal as only keyboard, mouse, screen updates and occasional print traffic travel over the network. Server Based Computing actually centralizes network traffic as the bulk of traffic flows between back-end systems, such as between Terminal Servers and email, web, database and file servers on the same or adjacent network. Server Based Computing and centralization of computing resources ensure that as little data as possible traverses over a network, promoting efficiencies in bandwidth management and bandwidth utilization and provide a positive and consistent user experience.

Figure 3.3 shows a Terminal Server environment hosting an email client. The actual client-server traffic that travels over the network is RDP not POP3.

Figure 3.3

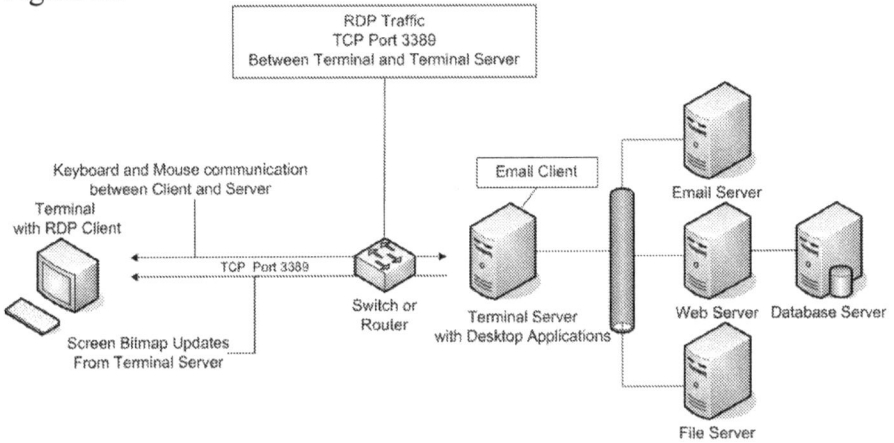

The above examples highlight the differences between the client-server model and Server Based Computing. They also show how Server Based Computing with Terminal Server complements and improves the performance and security of client-server applications by moving them from PCs to the data center where they can be centrally managed on a Terminal Server.

Traditional Networking Model
The traditional networking model leverages a centralized file server that is accessed directly by PCs. At the heart of the traditional network model is the network server that authenticates users and stores data or functions as a centrally located print server for the entire network. File and print services are available to client workstations (generally PCs) located on the local area network (LAN) or wide area network (WAN). Users would authenticate to a file and print server and the associated home directory and printer information would be established. Note that the traditional network model predates the concept of user domains. With the traditional network model, the processing is distributed between the PC and the server and PCs communicate directly with the file and print servers.

Figure 3.4 shows the traditional networking model.

Figure 3.4

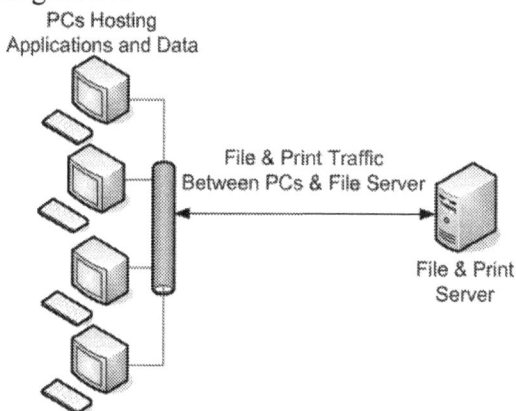

Client workstations can either download data files from a network server or open a data file on the file server. When the client accesses a file located on the server, the server's file system locks the file and makes it read only. This mechanism protects the data from being changed by more than one client at a time while it is being accessed. The client workstations run applications locally using local memory, processing, and hard drives. Clients essentially use the network server as a remote hard drive or network printer. A centralized print server allows a systems administrator to back up mission-critical data in one location rather than at each client workstation.

The traditional network model is common in small and mid-sized business environments because of its relative simplicity and minimal maintenance requirements. However, when the user population exceeds 100, performance decreases. The performance decreases are a result of the file server maintaining client connections via a "keep-alive" message service, even when no work is being performed. This model is very bandwidth intensive because of the traffic between the PC and server.

Traditional Networking Model with Terminal Server
The traditional networking model is enhanced by integrating domain authentication, authorization, file and print services in the form of

home directories, mapped network drives and network printing within a Terminal Server environment. Terminal Servers are placed next to the file server, reducing file access time and bandwidth utilization.

Terminal Server users can use what is referred to as a Terminal Server user profile. Terminal Server user profiles are configured globally within Active Directory and are an attribute of a Windows user account. A Terminal Server user profile contains user defaults such as home directory settings and logon scripts. After a user authenticates, the Terminal Server user profile establishes the user's environment by mapping his or her home directory, network shares, and network or locally attached printers, making them available from within the Terminal Server session.

The traditional networking model along with client-server, N-Tier, and Mainframes are a great fit for a Server Based Computing environment.

The next list highlights the pros and cons of Server Based Computing.

The **pros** of the Server Server-Based Computing are
- Provides a single entry point for users to all material systems into the corporate network.
- Provides visibility of all applications provisioned per a particular user.
- Offers centralized security configuration and monitoring.
- Offers centralized administration of applications and data.
- Upgrade and patch software from a central location.
- Leverages other computing models, such as client-server, N-tier, and traditional networking models.
- Offloads processing from desktop PCs to the Terminal Servers, allowing PCs to be replaced with Thin Clients.
- Is very scalable for accommodating large user populations.
- Employs off-the-shelf PC applications with little or no modification.
- Allows non-Windows machines to use Windows applications.
- Provides LAN-speed performance over low bandwidth connections.

The **cons** of the Server-Based Computing with Terminal Server are
- Requires additional server hardware.
- May require additional 3rd party load-balancing hardware to load balance Terminal Server farms.
- May increase server administration requirements as servers are added.

Chapter 3 Summary

This chapter discussed how Server Based Computing complements and improves the performance and security posture of N-tier, Traditional Networking, and Mainframe computing and concluded with the pros and cons of Server Based Computing.

Client-server & N-tier Models
- Client-server and N-tier computing models distribute application processing, data and network traffic between PCs and servers.
- The difference between client-server and N-tier is that client-server refers to legacy two tier applications, such as email and N-tier refers to multiple tier web applications.
- The Client-server Computing Model has been in use since the late 1980s and is widely adopted in the public and private sectors.
- In a client-server environment, client-server software is installed and maintained on the PC and local computing resources are used to run the client-server software.
- Terminal Server compliments and improves client-server computing by moving the client software, security controls and network traffic from PCs to a centrally managed Terminal Server environment.

Traditional Networking Model
- The traditional networking model leverages a centralized file server that is accessed directly by PCs.
- At the heart of the traditional network model is the network server that authenticates users and stores data files or functions as a centrally located print server for the entire network.

- The traditional network model is suitable for small and mid-size businesses where the user population starts at 11 and scales up to 100 networked users.
- The traditional networking model is improved by integrating domain authentication, authorization, file and print services in the form of home directories, mapped network drives, and network printing within a Terminal Server environment.

Chapter 4: Enterprise Architecture

Chapter Overview:
This chapter begins with a high level overview of Enterprise Architecture (EA) and concludes with an introduction to the Enterprise Architecture's policy infrastructure. Because Enterprise Architecture is a field unto itself, a detailed review of its principles, processes, and approach is beyond the scope of this book. The goal of this chapter is to explain how Terminal Server fits within an Enterprise Architecture.

The purpose of Enterprise Architecture is to establish an Enterprise wide blueprint used to achieve business objectives while maximizing the business value of information technology. An Enterprise Architecture is a "blueprint" that describes an organization's strategic direction, security and regulatory requirements, information technology portfolio and their inter-dependencies, baseline and target architectures, and the processes to implement new technologies. In business terms, Enterprise Architecture is accomplished by efficiently achieving an organization's mission with minimal investment in information technology; and in technical terms, by optimizing business operations, effective information technology planning, information technology budgeting, information technology acquisition, human resource utilization, and the implementation of security controls.

After the goals and stakeholders of an Enterprise Architecture project have been identified, a framework is selected to help implement and support the Enterprise Architecture through its entire life cycle. Frameworks provide methodologies, standards, guidelines, and formats that can be used as is or adapted to meet specific requirements. Because organizations have different missions and business objectives, no single framework will be right for each situation. Organizations typically select a framework or a mixture of frameworks to meet their requirements. There are a number of feasible frameworks, such as Cobit, ISO/IEC 17799, ITIL, and others that represents a variety of methodologies and toolsets to fulfill the requirements of any size or type of organization.

Enterprise Architecture has well defined principles and processes, along with an approach that generates a comprehensive layered policy infrastructure used to communicate management's goals, principles, instructions, appropriate procedures, and response to laws and regulatory mandates. A policy infrastructure consists of tier 1, tier 2 and tier 3 policies that encompass people, systems, data, and information. A policy infrastructure consists of policies, standards, procedures, baselines, and guidelines.

Tier 1 policies sit at the top of the policy infrastructure and address broad organizational issues, vision and direction. Most organizations will develop and support up to a dozen tier 1 policies. An example tier 1 policy is an Employee Practices Policy or a Conflict of Interest Policy. Global in scope, Tier 1 policies are high level documents that define vision and direction. Tier 2 policies are topic specific, and tier 3 policies are application or system specific. Standards are tier 2 policies that describe system design concepts, implementation steps, and detailed configurations. Procedures are tier 2 & 3 policies that provide step by step compulsory measures, communicating best practices in using information systems and organizational data/information. Baselines are tier 3 policies that are application or system specific and describe step by step instructions to implement technologies. Guidelines are tier 3 documents, offering application, system, or procedural specific best practices. Guidelines are recommendations unlike policies, standards, procedures, and baselines, which are compulsory.

Figure 4.1 shows the organization of Enterprise Architecture's layered policy infrastructure.

Figure 4.1

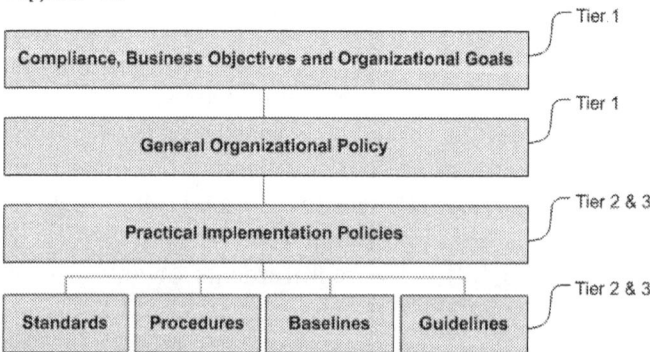

56

Figure 4.1 represents Enterprise Architecture's layered policy infrastructure, starting with tier 1 policies which address broad organizational issues, vision, and direction. The next layer, General Organizational Policy, consists of tier 1 policies in which management makes security statements, explains roles and responsibilities, and defines which assets are considered valuable. The following layer, Practical Implementation Policies, contains tier 2 and 3 policies which are topic, application, and system specific and are used to enforce upper layer policies. The lower layer consists of tier 2 and 3 policies which are topic and technology specific and are used to enforce higher layer policies.

Figure 4.2 shows the work flow of a policy infrastructure.

Figure 4.2

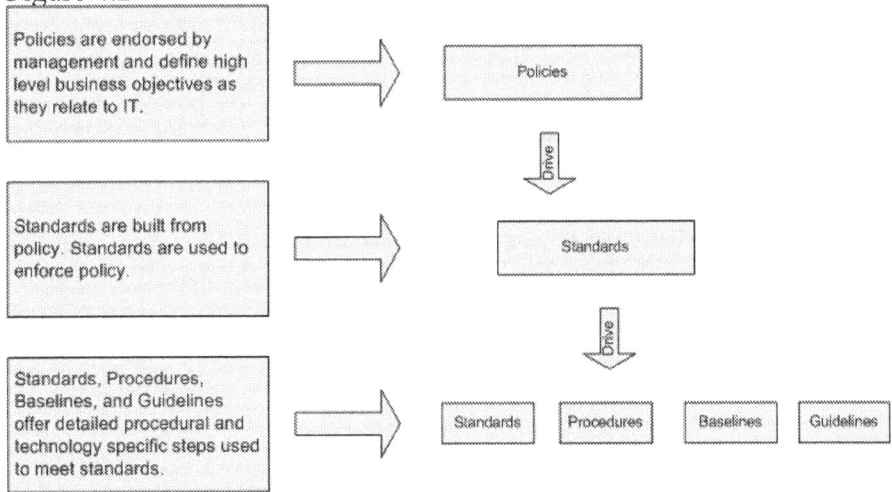

A policy infrastructure contains confidential information relating to running a business and the publication, distribution and storage of that information should be strictly monitored. Many organizations leverage the human resource department and web-based intranet solutions to distribute and control access to policies.

An Enterprise Architecture groups infrastructure components within topic specific domains. An example of Enterprise Architecture domains are infrastructure, applications, network, and security. After an organization has defined its Enterprise Architecture domains, all infrastructure components are grouped within their corresponding domain and reviewed individually and as a single cohesive unit. Layered policies are developed for each domain and individual technology within a domain.

Table 4.1 shows the Enterprise Architecture domain structure that will be used throughout this book. The example encompasses five domains split between two high level domains of infrastructure and applications. The domains are platform, network, software, data / information, and security.

Table 4.1

Enterprise Architecture Scope	
Infrastructure	**Applications**
Platform	Software
Network	Data/Information
Security	

An organization's mission and business objectives drive its Enterprise Architecture domain structure. As we have all learned, there is no 'one size fits all' with information technology, and Enterprise Architecture is no exception. Enterprise Architecture is flexible and can be molded to suit any organization's mission and business objectives.

Table 4.2 shows a variation of the above Enterprise Architecture domain structure.

Table 4.2

Enterprise Architecture Scope
Platform
Network
Software
Data/Information
Security
Access Domain
Integration Domain
Privacy Domain
Project Management Domain
Systems Management Domain

Each of the domains within an Enterprise Architecture will have its corresponding layered policy infrastructure, with tier 1 & 2 policies, tier 2 & 3 standards, procedures, baselines, and guidelines. Many of the layered policies within an Enterprise Architecture govern a Terminal Server environment because they dictate user access methods, network infrastructure parameters, and applications and security controls that work within a Terminal Server environment.

To gain a broader understanding of how Terminal Server fits within an Enterprise Architecture, the next sections will review tier 2 & 3 policies from the platform, network, software, data/information, and security domains.

Platform Architecture Domain
The platform architecture domain defines the roles, policies, standards, and decision-making criteria for the acquisition and deployment of all computing and data storage hardware and operating systems for servers, desktops, and handheld devices. The platform architecture domain policies start with a definition of high level platform architecture requirements and cascade down to hardware standards and operating system installation and configuration. High level policies from the platform architecture domain include the Platform Architecture Policy and Platform Infrastructure Standard, which establish the foundation for lower layer policies.

List 4.1 shows a partial list of the layered policies within the platform architecture domain.
- Platform Architecture Policy
- Platform Infrastructure Standard
- Server Standards
- Windows Terminal Server Standards
- Windows Server Security Policy
- Hardware Virtualization Standards

Note: An organization's policy infrastructure directly reflects its unique mission and business objectives. The above list is for educational purposes only.

At the top of the platform architecture domain policy infrastructure sits the Platform Architecture Policy. The Platform Architecture Policy is a big picture tier 2, non vendor specific document, which establishes high level platform architecture requirements that define the acquisition and deployment of servers, end-user devices, and storage technologies. Lower level tier 3 policies define vendor specific technologies, outlining system-specific or procedural-specific standards and requirements.

Many of the lower level tier 3 policies define the controls that govern the acquisition and deployment of the hardware and operating system upon which Terminal Server will run. They also define data storage and personal computing devices requirements. During the development and periodic review of platform architecture policies, Terminal Server and supporting technologies must be carefully considered to ensure interoperability, integration, and security.

The next example is a platform architecture policy. The goal with this example is to illustrate the relationship between a high level tier 2 platform architecture policy and Terminal Server. This policy is intended for informational purposes only.

Platform Architecture Policy

Purpose and Scope
The purpose of this policy is to establish platform architecture requirements which control the acquisition, use, and management of server, personal computing devices, and storage technologies. This policy provides controls that ensure Enterprise issues are considered along with business objectives when making computing platform related decisions. The scope of the platforms in this policy includes servers, personal computing devices and storage systems.

Platform Architecture policies, standards and guidelines will be used to acquire, design and implement servers, personal computing devices, and storage systems.

Responsibilities

The CEO and CIO ensure that policies are followed in order to establish contracts, review procurement requests and to develop and manage services.

Platform Architecture Goals

The goals to employ computing platform controls are to:

- Ensure that platform devices support industry-wide open-standards and seamlessly interoperate with other platform devices, operating systems, storage technologies and embedded security.
- Meet business objectives through greater efficiencies in the acquisition and use of computing platforms.
- Ensure the availability of tools in order to meet business objectives, security, management and productivity requirements.

Platform Architecture Categories

Platform Architecture categories address servers, personal computing devices and storage technologies, including their hardware and operating systems. Platform Architecture categories include Servers, Personal Computing Devices, and Storage.

Servers

A server is a computer that provides services for other computers. Types of servers include:

- Mainframe servers
- High-end servers
- Mid-range to small servers

Personal Computing Devices

Personal computing devices are desktop computers, thin clients, laptops and handheld devices, including the operating systems and their hardware. Types of personal computing devices include:

- Desktop personal computers
- Thin Clients
- Handheld devices

Storage

Storage technologies address short term, long term and permanent storage of information and data. Types of storage technologies include:

- Direct Attached Storage
- Network Attached Storage
- Storage Area Network

Assumptions and Expectations

Platform Architecture evaluates platform technologies in terms of flexibility, scalability, and interoperability with other platform technologies and operating systems. Each platform architecture category should have the following characteristics: Servers, Personal Computing Devices and Storage.

Servers

- Have embedded security
- Support industry-wide open-standards
- Support centralized management
- Support common management tools
- Interoperate with other platform technologies

Personal Computing Devices

- Have embedded security
- Support industry-wide open-standards
- Support centralized management
- Support common management tools
- Interoperate with other platform technologies

Storage

- Have security
- Support industry-wide open-standards
- Support centralized storage
- Support common management tools
- Interoperate with other platform technologies

Compliance

All information technology investments will comply with existing policies to ensure the integrity and interoperability of computing platforms.

Related Policies

Platform Infrastructure Standard

The example Platform Architecture Policy illustrates how a policy is used to define high level computing platform requirements, roles and responsibilities. The policy defines servers, personal computing devices and data storage computing platform requirements. Each individual computing platform must have seamless interoperability and integration with Terminal Server. During the development or review of platform architecture policy, Terminal Server and other computing platforms must be carefully considered to ensure interoperability, integration and security.

Summary

The platform architecture domain defines the roles, policies, standards and decision-making criteria for the acquisition and deployment of all computing and data storage hardware and operating systems for servers, desktops and handheld devices.

Network Architecture Domain

The network architecture domain defines the network infrastructure and explains how data flows between systems, computers and devices on a network. It defines the technologies used to enable reliable, secure communication on LAN, WAN and wireless networks. Architects that develop or review network architecture policies must understand Terminal Server architecture and end-user access requirements in order to ensure reliable and available network access to resources via Terminal Server.

List 4.2 shows a partial list of the layered policies within the network architecture domain.
- Network Architecture Policy
- Network Infrastructure Standard

- Router and Switch Technology Standards
- Network Security Standards

Note: The policy infrastructure of an organization directly reflects the unique mission and business objectives of the organization. The above list is for educational purposes only.

Network infrastructure enables reliable and secure communication between information systems and all related computing platforms. The network architecture domain with its layered policies takes into consideration Terminal Server architectural and supporting computing platforms to ensure reliable and secure communications over a wide variety of networks.

The next example is an abbreviated network architecture policy. The goal with this example is to illustrate the relationship between a high level network architecture policy and Terminal Server. This policy is intended for informational purposes only.

Network Architecture Policy

Purpose and Scope
The purpose of this policy is to establish network architecture requirements that describe how information processing resources are interconnected to topology standards, transport media, and protocols used to deliver converged services, including traditional data, voice, and video services. This policy provides controls that ensure Enterprise issues are considered along with business objectives when making network architecture related decisions. The scope of the architecture in this policy includes a network infrastructure to enable converged services, such as traditional data, voice and video services.

Responsibilities
The CEO and CIO ensure that policies are followed in order to establish contracts and procurement requests and to develop and manage services.

Network Architecture Goals

The goals to employ network architecture controls are:

- Networks should be operational, reliable and available 24x7x365 to support mission-critical business operations and processes.
- Networks should be designed for security, growth and adaptability.
- Network architecture shall use proven open industry standards.
- Network architecture will support converged services while accommodating traditional data, voice and video services.

Network Architecture Topology

Network architecture topology consists of the following:

- Local Area Network (LAN): A local area network is a communications system that covers a small local area, like an office or building.
- Wide Area Network (WAN): A wide area network is a communications system that spans a large geographical area.

Network architecture transport media include:

- Wired (i.e. copper, fiber)
- Wireless (i.e. 802.x, all EVDO)

Network Architecture protocols provide the rules that support network access and communication.

Assumptions and Expectations

Network Architecture evaluates network technologies in terms of flexibility, scalability, and interoperability with other technologies.

Compliance

All information technology investments shall conform to existing policies in order to ensure the integrity and interoperability of computing platforms.

Related Policies
Network Architecture Standard
Network Architecture Guideline

The example network architecture policy illustrates how a policy is used to define network architecture requirements and to describe how information processing resources are interconnected.

Summary
Unlike the platform architecture domain policies that govern Terminal Server, the network architecture domain establishes the foundation to plan, build, run and monitor the network infrastructure. Architects that oversee the development or review of network architecture policy must understand Terminal Server architecture and end-user access requirements to ensure reliable and available network access to resources via Terminal Server.

The next section will review the data and information architecture domain. We will also review a data classification and categorization standard which is used to define the classification and categorization of data/information and information systems such as Terminal Server.

Data/ Information Architecture Domain
The data/information architecture domain provides the layered policy infrastructure that describes business processes, data requirements of business systems and user data, and the classification and categorization of data/information and information systems. High level policies, such as the Data Architecture Policy, describe the requirements used to develop, acquire and implement technologies that collect, modify, store and report data/information. Other high level policies within the data and information architecture domain are the Data Modeling Standards, used to develop flow charts to understand business processes and data flow, and the Data/Information Classification and Categorization Standards, which are used as a framework to define data/information's criticality and sensitivity levels, custodian responsibilities and accessibility.

List 4.3 shows a partial list of the layered policies within the data/information architecture domain.

- Data Architecture Policy
- Data Modeling Standards
- Data/Information Classification and Categorization Standards
- Database Systems Standards
- Data Modeling Standards
- Enterprise Document Management System Standards

Note: The policy infrastructure of an organization directly reflects the unique mission and business objectives of the organization. The above list is for educational purposes only.

Policies from the data and information architecture domain lay the foundation for information security by explaining business processes and how information flows between systems. The data and information architecture domain will also provide guidance for personnel on how to classify and maintain data. Data classification and maintenance policies allow organizations to implement the appropriate security controls based on the sensitivity and criticality of data/information.

Terminal Server is often used as the primary interface to applications, data and information. From a data/information security perspective, security controls will be implemented at multiple layers (defense in depth), starting with compartmentalization of data and systems along with administrative and technical security controls.

The next example is an abbreviated Data/Information Classification and Categorization Standard. This example shows how a standard allows an organization to define data/information classifications and security levels for both data/information and information systems. This standard is intended for informational purposes only.

Data/Information Classification and Categorization Standard

Purpose and Scope
The purpose of this standard is to identify classifications and security levels for all forms of data/information and information systems across the Enterprise. It is intended to establish a "need to know" data/information classification methodology in order to protect

<Company Name> data and information against unauthorized discloser, loss or misuse. This standard provides controls that ensure Enterprise issues are considered along with business objectives when making data/information classification decisions. The scope of the standard covers all forms of <Company Name> data/information throughout its entire life cycle, from its origination to its destruction.

Data Classification Standards Goals

The goals of this standard is to establish how data/information is classified according to its criticality and sensitivity and to ensure that <Company Name> data/information preserves its security classification as it traverses information systems or non-electronic boundaries.

Data Classifications

All <Company Name> information will be categorized into three main classifications:

- Public
- Internal
- Confidential

Table 1 provides examples of each classification and required security measure.

Table 1

Security Objective	Data Classification		
	Public	**Internal**	**Confidential**
Criteria		Unauthorized disclosure would not considerably impact organization.	Unauthorized disclosure would result in considerable adverse impact, embarrassment or legal actions.
Examples	Examples include public web site, press	Examples include inter-office	Examples include employee records, department

	releases, marketing brochures, annual reports, and public financial filings.	memoranda, internal correspond-dence, employee newsletters, internal directories, and internal policies.	financial data, purchasing information, new product designs, strategic plans, marketing studies, vendor and customer contracts, confidential information of organizations customers, partners, and suppliers.
Accessibility	Available to the general public, can be distributed outside the organization.	Available for internal use. May be shared outside the organization to meet business objectives only when approved by a manager.	Access is limited to a "need to know" basis within the organization.
Document Label	None	"Internal"	"Confidential"

Data and information, regardless of its medium, will be:
- Classified as either public, internal, or confidential.
- Used in a manner equivalent with its classification.
- Segregated by accessibility, file structure, or presentation.
- Secured in accordance with applicable standards.
- Disposed of in accordance with applicable standards.

Data and Information Custodians Responsibilities
Data/information custodians are responsible for the classification and execution of security controls of data they own, create or have become

a delegate of. Data and information custodians retain their responsibility of data classification and execution of security controls for data and information within the organization, or for data/information that is shared with other organizations.

Security Categories for Data/Information and Information Systems

Source: FIPS PUB 199-final, Categorization of Information and Information Systems.

This section establishes security categories for both data/information and information systems. The security categories are based on the potential impact on an organization should certain events occur that jeopardize the information and information systems needed by the organization to accomplish its assigned mission, protect its assets, fulfill its legal responsibilities, maintain its day-to-day functions and protect individuals. Security categories are to be used in conjunction with vulnerability and threat information in assessing the risk to an organization.

Categorization of data/information and software application systems includes risk levels of confidentiality, integrity, and availability. Table 2 summarizes the security objectives and their risk levels.

Table 2

POTENTIAL IMPACT			
Security Objective	**LOW**	**MODERATE**	**HIGH**
Confidentiality Preserving authorized restrictions on information access and disclosure, including means for protecting personal privacy and proprietary information. [44 U.S.C., SEC. 3542]	The unauthorized disclosure of information could be expected to have a **limited** adverse effect on organizational operations, organizational assets or individuals.	The unauthorized disclosure of information could be expected to have a **serious** adverse effect on organizational operations, organizational assets or individuals.	The unauthorized disclosure of information could be expected to have a **severe or catastrophic** adverse effect on organizational operations, organizational assets or individuals.
Integrity Guarding against improper information modification or destruction; includes ensuring information non-repudiation and authenticity. [44 U.S.C., SEC. 3542]	The unauthorized modification or destruction of information could be expected to have a **limited** adverse effect on organizational operations, organizational assets or individuals.	The unauthorized modification or destruction of information could be expected to have a **serious** adverse effect on organizational operations, organizational assets or individuals.	The unauthorized modification or destruction of information could be expected to have a **severe or catastrophic** adverse effect on organizational operations, organizational assets or individuals.
Availability Ensuring timely and reliable access to and use of information. [44 U.S.C., SEC. 3542]	The disruption of access to or use of information or an information system could be expected to have a **limited** adverse effect on organizational operations, organizational assets or individuals.	The disruption of access to or use of information or an information system could be expected to have a **serious** adverse effect on organizational operations, organizational assets or individuals.	The disruption of access to or use of information or an information system could be expected to have a **severe or catastrophic** adverse effect on organizational operations, organizational assets or individuals.

The potential impact is LOW if the loss of confidentiality, integrity or availability could be expected to have a limited adverse effect on organizational operations, organizational assets or individuals.

The potential impact is MODERATE if the loss of confidentiality, integrity or availability could be expected to have a serious adverse effect on organizational operations, organizational assets or individuals.

The potential impact is HIGH if the loss of confidentiality, integrity or availability could be expected to have a severe or catastrophic adverse effect on organizational operations, organizational assets or individuals.

Compliance
All classification and security levels for data/information and information systems will conform to existing policies. Any employee found to have violated this standard may be subject to disciplinary action, up to and including termination of employment.

Related Policies
Data Architecture Policy
Data Modeling Standards
Data Security Policy

Reference
FIPS PUB 199-final

The example illustrates how a standard defines classifications and security levels for all forms of data/information and information systems across the Enterprise. The classification of data/information and information systems sets the stage for information security, allowing organizations to employ the appropriate security control based on the sensitivity or criticality of data and information systems.

Summary
The data and information architecture domain directly influences the design, support and auditing of a Terminal Server environment. Organizations implement administrative and technical controls to

ensure the confidentiality, integrity and availability of sensitive data. From a design perspective, Terminal Server silos can be leveraged to support access to different data security levels. One Terminal Server silo with one set of security controls can be leveraged to access internal data, while other silos with different security controls such as encryption and application access restrictions are used to access confidential data. Terminal Server silos allow the appropriate security controls such as auditing and encryption to be implemented based on the sensitivity of the data or application accessed from a given Terminal Server silo.

Software Architecture Domain

The software architecture domain defines the methodologies, tools and best practices to develop, acquire, deploy and retire software that automates and maintains business processes. It provides a framework to ensure the integrity, interoperability and integration of software and computing platforms. The software architecture domain policy infrastructure provides the framework to support the entire lifecycle of software, including desktop applications and management software installed and managed on Terminal Servers. Software architecture can consist of the following components:

1. Applications
   o Software designed to automate specific business processes, such as customer resource management, employee services, accounts payable, payroll, etc.
2. Programming Software
   o Enabling technologies used to develop software.
3. Database Software
   o Database management systems that enable organizations to store, modify and extract information from a database.
4. Productivity Software
   o Office productivity and collaborative software.
5. Management Software
   o Software used to maintain, monitor and audit network infrastructure and computing platforms.

An example of high level tier 2 policy in the software architecture domain is the Software Architecture Policy, which describes high level requirements to design, develop or acquire software. Another example high level policy is a tier 2 Applications and Software Standard that is used to describe high level application and software standards. Lower level tier 2 & 3 policies describe individual applications or application groups. An example would be the Productivity Application Standards, which is a tier 2 policy describing Enterprise-wide productivity application standards. Lower level tier 3 policies describe application A, B or C's configuration and use.

List 4.4 shows a partial list of the layered policies within the software architecture domain.
- Software Architecture Policy
- Application and Software Standards
- Productivity Application Standards
- Application Development Standards
- Load and Performance Testing Software Standards
- Software Licensing Policy

Note: The policy infrastructure of an organization directly reflects the unique mission and business objectives of the organization. The above list is for educational purposes only.

The next example is a tier 3 Terminal Server Application Software Policy. This example illustrates the relationship between the software architecture domain, layered policy infrastructure and Terminal Server. This policy is intended for informational purposes only.

Terminal Server Application Software Policy

Purpose and Scope
The purpose of this policy is to define Terminal Server application software requirements that control the acquisition, use, management and retirement of software applications. This policy provides controls that ensure that Enterprise issues are considered along with business objectives when making Terminal Server application software related decisions.

The scope of this policy includes all standard desktop suites and application software intended for use on Terminal Servers.

Responsibilities

The CEO and CIO ensure that policies are followed to establish contracts, review procurement requests and to develop and manage services.

Policy Identifies and Defines

- Define <Company Name's> Terminal Server desktop and list all supported application software.
- Define a standard model for deployment, installation and updates of Terminal Server application software.
- Define each application software's life cycle, classification and management requirements.

Standard Desktop and Sanctioned Application Software

The standard desktop is available exclusively from <Company Name> Terminal Servers. The standard desktop will contain approved desktop suites and application software as a business service for the purpose of supporting <Company Name> business activities and occasional personal use as defined in the Acceptable Use Policy.

The standard Terminal Server desktop application portfolio will consist of the following categories:

a. Office Productivity

- Word processor
- Spreadsheet
- Presentational software
- Customer Relations Management software
- Project management software
- Email client with group calendaring and address book facility
- Web browser with essential plug-ins
- Media player
- PDF reader
- File compression/archiving tool
- File browser
- Calculator

b. Management Software
- Anti-virus and malware software
- Log Analyzer
- Network sensor

c. Optional Software
- "in-house" software
- Graphics editing
- Web authoring
- PDF writer
- Terminal emulation client
- X-Windows client

This list contains application software that is specifically prohibited:
- Games
- Peer to peer file sharing software
- FTP software
- Instant messaging clients

The names and versions of software in the above categories are found in the Application Software Standards document.

Application Software Deployment
- <Company Name> IT staff will provide an automated standard deployment solution for application software. This model will be used to deploy and update all software on the standard desktop.
- All application software intended for deployment on the standard desktop will first require "packaging". <Company Name> IT staff will provide a packaging solution for this purpose. When it is not technically possible to package an application, an alternative will be presented to management for approval before the application is put into production.

Application Software Life Cycle Classification and Management Requirements
The application software life cycle classifications are: current, contained, retired and research/emerging. The classifications are defined in the Application Software Standards policy.

Application software life cycle management follows NIST Special Publication 800-64 and is defined in the Systems Life Cycle Management Policy.

Assumptions and Expectations

Terminal Server Application Software will be evaluated in terms of cost, flexibility, scalability and interoperability with Terminal Server and other platform technologies. Each Terminal Server Application Software category should have the following characteristics:

- Embedded security and logging capabilities
- Support for industry-wide open-standards
- Support for centralized management
- Interoperation with other platform technologies and authentication systems

Application Software Approval Process

Before any application software is put into production, it will go through an approval process. Before any application software is approved for production, an Application Assessment Profile (Appendix A) is submitted for approval.

Appendix A

Application Assessment Profile

Survey Site:		Date:		Surveyor:	
Application:		Version:		Type:	
Install directory:		Install date:			
User(s):					
Describe the application function:					
Application manufacturer:		Manufacturer contact(s):			
Manufacturer Web:		Manufacturer phone:			
Questions:		Answer:		Comments:	
ISV or custom-built application?					

If custom-built, is the source code available?		
Is the vendor still in business?		
How often is this application used?		
How many users use this application?		
Does the application require a DOS device driver?		
Does the application require any input devices besides a keyboard and mouse? Please describe how the devices are attached.		
Does the application use .ini files? If so, please provide details.		
How much memory does the application require?		
Does the application depend on DCOM?		
Does the application require IPX?		
Will the application work with IP?		
Does the application require a unique IP address to work?		
Does the application have a dependency on a server component? If so, is there a set of api that it uses?		
Is there a database dependency? What database/version?		
Is there a host connectivity dependency? If so, what kind (appc, nfs)?		

What is the data flow for the application?		
Would you consider this a graphic-intensive application?		
Describe other application dependencies.		
Is the version of the software the latest version available?		
Is this a custom Windows NT graphical identification and authentication (GINA) DLL?		

Compliance

All Terminal Server Application Software shall conform to existing policies. Any employee found to have violated this policy may be subject to disciplinary action, up to and including termination of employment.

Related Policies

Acceptable Use Policy
Application Software Standards
Systems Life Cycle Management Policy

Reference

NIST Special Publication 800-64

The example illustrates how a policy defines the application software life cycle for a Terminal Server environment. This policy provides the foundation for lower level policies that are used to design, develop, implement and maintain application software on Terminal Servers.

Summary

The software architecture domain defines the methodologies, tools and best practices in order to develop, acquire, deploy and retire application software. It provides a framework to ensure the integrity, interoperability and integration of application software and computing platforms across the Enterprise. The software architecture domain policy infrastructure provides the framework to support the entire lifecycle of application software. Architects that oversee the development or review of software architecture policy must understand Terminal Server application software requirements to ensure the integrity, interoperability and integration of application software in a Terminal Server environment.

Security Architecture Domain

The security architecture domain defines the roles, policies and process reviews to implement and monitor security across an Enterprise. The security architecture domain encompasses people, physical security and the technologies used for security management, such as surveillance, firewalls, intrusion detection, cryptography, public key infrastructure (PKI), authentication, authorization, remote access, virus detection, and so forth. It enables organizations to look at their entire technology portfolio as a single cohesive unit and apply the appropriate security controls in order to achieve business objectives without compromising user productivity.

An example of a high level policy in the security architecture domain is the Security Architecture Policy, which defines security and regulatory requirements used to establish a recommended minimum security architecture baseline. Another example of high level policy is the IT Risk Management Standard that defines a Risk Management process.

List 4.5 shows a partial list of the layered policies within the security architecture domain.
- IT Risk Management Standard
- Change Management Policy
- Incident Response Policy
- Encryption Standard
- IT Disaster Recovery Planning Policy
- IT Physical Security Standard

Note: The policy infrastructure of an organization directly reflects the unique mission and business objectives of the organization. The above list is for educational purposes only.

There are many policies within the security architecture domain that govern a Terminal Server environment. Security controls, such as physical and environmental policies, encryption standards, authentication, authorization, Anti-Virus Guidelines, server hardening, and so forth, are applied to Terminal Servers via the security architecture domain policy infrastructure.

The next two examples introduce a tier 3 Terminal Server Anti-Virus Software Guideline, followed by a tier 2 Change Management Policy. These examples illustrate the relationship between the security architecture domain's layered policy infrastructure and Terminal Server.

Even with the most state of the art content filtering system, firewall, and proxy server rules, viruses find their way into the environment. Anti-virus software is a necessity in contemporary computing environments in order to protect hosts from malware and to meet legal and regulatory mandates.

Anti-virus software scans active processes in memory and files while comparing them against a database of known signatures. Most anti-virus solutions protect against all three types of malware - spyware, spam and viruses. Unfortunately, the protection is only as good as the signature database which must be kept up to date to detect the latest types of malware.

This guideline is intended for informational purposes only.

Terminal Server Anti-virus Software Guidelines
The following list introduces guidelines to acquire, implement and configure anti-virus software on Terminal Server:
- Select an anti-virus solution that enables updated signatures to be pulled from an internal source. This provides an opportunity to validate new signatures in a lab before deploying them into production.

- Select an anti-virus solution that allows virus definitions to be updated without rebooting the server.
- Select an anti-virus solution that allows the status icon in the system tray to be disabled. Typically, the status icon in the system tray is disabled by removing a value from the HKEY_LOCAL_MACHINE\Software\Micrrosoft\Windows\CurrentVersion\Run registry key.
- Select an anti-virus solution that allows scans of every file on the system to be scheduled during off-hours.

The proceeding Terminal Server Anti-Virus Software Guidelines show how an organization uses a guideline to suggest best practices and to acquire, implement and configure anti-virus software for Terminal Servers. Unlike tier 2 and 3 policies and standards, guidelines are not obligatory, but they are suggested best practices.

The next example is a tier 2 Change Management Policy. This policy is intended for informational purposes only.

Change Management Policy

Overview
Changes require careful planning, testing and monitoring to reduce negative impact to user productivity. Change management exists to coordinate and inform personnel of all changes that impact any computing system or service. The purpose of change management is to insure that technical requirements are clearly defined, documented, scheduled and controlled throughout the product life cycle. The overriding goal is to provide a high level of availability and service.

Purpose and Scope
The purpose of this policy is to establish change management processes in order to manage changes to hardware, software, firmware and documentation in a coherent and predictable manner so personnel can plan accordingly. This policy provides controls that ensure Enterprise issues are considered along with business objectives when changing hardware, software, firmware and documentation. The scope of the policy includes all hardware, software, firmware and

documentation. The Change Management Policy applies to all individuals who install, manage or maintain information resources.

Change Management procedures:

Any change to information resources will comply with the Change Management Policy and will follow the change management procedures.

A. A formal written change request will be submitted to the CIO before any change, either scheduled or unscheduled, containing the following information:
1. Change Description: A technical description of the change.
2. Change Purpose: A technical description of the purpose of the change.
3. Change Testing: List the completed QA testing.
4. Role-back Procedures: A technical description of the role-back procedures.
5. Timing: A detailed schedule when the change will take place.
6. Responsibilities: A list of the personnel, their responsibilities, and their contact information for those who are involved in the implementation of the change.
7. Impact Analysis: An impact analysis on change.

B. All changes will be maintained in a Change Management log that contains:
1. Date of change
2. Responsible parties contact information
3. Nature of the change
4. Indication of success or failure

Assumptions and Expectations

All information systems must comply with the change management policy and meet the procedures outlined above.

Compliance

Any employee found to have violated this policy may be subject to disciplinary action, up to and including termination of employment.

The example illustrates how a policy defines the change management procedures for an organizations hardware, software, firmware and documentation.

Chapter 4 Summary

This chapter discussed Enterprise Architecture and reviewed example policies from five Enterprise Architecture domains: Platform Architecture Domain, Network Architecture Domain, Data/ Information Architecture Domain, Software Architecture Domain and the Security Architecture Domain. The goal of the chapter is to demonstrate the interrelations between Enterprise Architecture, a policy infrastructure and Terminal Server.

Enterprise Architecture
- An Enterprise Architecture defines an Enterprise-wide blueprint that describes strategic direction, business requirements, information technology portfolio, architectures and the processes to implement new technologies.
- Enterprise Architecture has established principles, processes that are expressed within a policy infrastructure used to communicate management's goals, principles, instructions and appropriate procedures and response to laws and regulatory mandates.
- A policy infrastructure consists of tier 1, tier 2 and tier 3 policies that consist of policies, standards, procedures, baselines and guidelines.
- Once the goals and stakeholders of an Enterprise Architecture project are identified, a framework is selected to help with implementation and life cycle management.
- Frameworks provide methodologies, standards, guidelines and formats that can be used as is or adapted to meet specific business requirements (i.e. Cobit, ISO/IEC 17799, ITIL, etc.).
- All infrastructure components are grouped within their corresponding Enterprise Architecture domain and reviewed individually and together as a single cohesive unit. Layered policies are developed for each domain and individual technology within a domain.

Platform Architecture Domain
- The platform architecture domain defines the roles, policies, standards and decision-making criteria for the acquisition and deployment of all computing and data storage hardware and operating systems for servers, desktops and handheld devices.
- Lower level tier 3 policies define the controls that govern the acquisition and deployment of the hardware and operating system that Terminal Server will run.

Network Architecture Domain
- The network architecture domain defines the network infrastructure and explains how data flows between systems, computers and devices on a network.
- The network architecture domain with its layered policies takes into consideration Terminal Server and architectural and supporting computing platforms to ensure reliable and secure communications over a wide variety of networks.

Data/ Information Architecture Domain
- The data/information architecture domain provides the layered policy infrastructure describing business processes; data requirements of business systems and user data; and classification and categorization of data/information and information systems.
- Policies from the data and information architecture domain lay the foundation for information security by explaining business processes and how information flows between systems.
- The data and information architecture domain provides guidance on how to classify and maintain data.

The Software Architecture Domain
- The software architecture domain defines the methodologies, tools and best practices to develop, acquire, deploy and retire software that automates and maintains business processes.
- The software architecture domain policy infrastructure provides the framework to support the entire lifecycle of

software, including desktop applications and management software installed and managed on Terminal Servers.

Security Architecture Domain
- The security architecture domain defines the roles, policies and process reviews to implement and monitor security across an Enterprise.
- The security architecture domain encompasses people, physical security and the technologies used for security management.
- It enables organizations to look at their entire technology portfolio as a single, cohesive unit and to apply the appropriate security controls in order to achieve business objectives without compromising user productivity.

The next chapter will introduce Enterprise Security Architecture and infrastructure design concepts.

Resources:
Federal CIO Council Website:
http://www.cio.gov/index.cfm?function=documents
Government Information Technology Agency
http://gita.state.az.us/about_gita/
Commonwealth of Pennsylvania, Office of Administration
http://www.oit.state.pa.us/oaoit/site/default.asp
Texas Department of Information Resources
http://www.dir.state.tx.us/management/index.htm

Chapter 5: Enterprise Security Architecture

Chapter Overview:
This chapter will introduce Enterprise Security Architecture (ESA), beginning with an introduction of Enterprise Security Architecture and Risk Management and a review of a Risk Assessment Policy, followed by an Enterprise Security Policy. Next we will highlight Enterprise Security Architecture infrastructure design concepts: defense in depth, the principle of least privilege, compartmentalization of information, and security domains. The chapter will conclude with two example network topologies, highlighting the Enterprise Security Architecture infrastructure design concepts in this chapter. The goal of this chapter is to show how Enterprise Security Architecture design concepts with Terminal Server can be used to provide secure access to different classifications of data, applications and users.

Enterprise Security Architecture introduces Risk Management techniques, methodologies and practices used to secure today's complex Enterprise. Enterprise Security Architecture is an integral component of an Enterprise Architecture and an information security program. Enterprise Architecture provides the foundation to develop and deploy technologies, while Enterprise Security Architecture is used as a guideline in making strategic, architectural security decisions.

Note: Because Enterprise Security Architecture and Risk Management are separate and distinct disciplines, a detailed discourse is beyond the scope of this book. I will, therefore, delve only into the details that are most relevant.

Risk Management & Risk Assessments
The goal of Risk Management is to protect the organization and its ability to achieve its mission. Risk Management is a process that provides a framework to enable people and organizations to assess risk and develop strategies to manage it. Risk Management strategies

include transferring risk to others, risk avoidance, minimizing the negative effect of risk or accepting risk. A Risk Assessment is a step in the Risk Management process that can be used to assess a specific risk. An information security Risk Assessment is used to determine areas of vulnerability within the IT environment to initiate remediation.

Figure 5.1 shows the elements of a Risk Assessment.

Figure 5.1

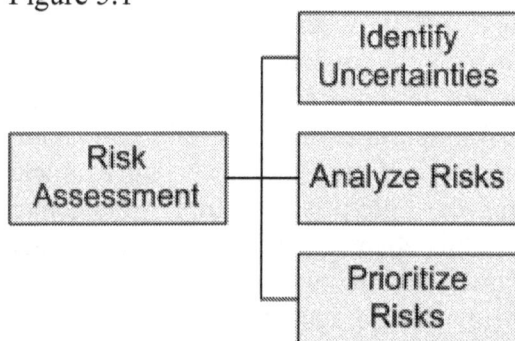

In terms of information security, there are many advantages in using Risk Management and Risk Assessments. The advantages are the ability to identify, quantify and manage risk along with cost justification. Many IT organizations leverage Risk Assessments to educate management on security awareness and to justify spending to shore up the security posture of their environments.

Tip: In terms of assessing Information Technology risk, evaluate the NIST Special Publication 800-30, *Risk Management Guide to Information Technology Systems*. It is a detailed guide on how to conduct a Risk Assessment and determine suitable technical, management and operational security controls.

The following example is a Risk Assessment Policy from the SANS Policy Project. It is used to sanction InfoSec to perform periodic information security Risk Assessments (RAs) in order to determine areas of vulnerability, and when applicable, to initiate remediation. This policy is intended for informational purposes only.

Risk Assessment Policy

Purpose
To empower InfoSec to perform periodic information security risk assessments (RAs) for the purpose of determining areas of vulnerability and to initiate appropriate remediation.

Scope
Risk assessments can be conducted on any entity within <Company Name> or any outside entity that has signed a Third Party Agreement with <Company Name>. RAs can be conducted on any information system, to include applications, servers and networks, and any process or procedure by which these systems are administered and/or maintained.

Policy
The execution, development and implementation of remediation programs are the joint responsibility of InfoSec and the department responsible for the systems area being assessed. Employees are expected to cooperate fully with any RA being conducted on systems for which they are held accountable. Employees are further expected to work with the InfoSec Risk Assessment Team in the development of a remediation plan.

Compliance
Any employee found to have violated this policy may be subject to disciplinary action, up to and including termination of employment.

Summary
The proceeding Risk Assessment Policy was presented to demonstrate how organizations use policy to communicate management's endorsement of InfoSec in order to perform a Risk Assessment. The policy states that InfoSec can conduct a Risk Assessment on any entity within the organization or on any outside entity that has signed a Third Party Agreement. The execution, development and implementation of remediation will be a joint engagement between InfoSec and the department responsible for the assessed systems.

The next section will review an Enterprise Security Policy. An Enterprise Security Policy is used to bridge the gap between technical and administrative security controls used together to instruct employees and business partners on how to securely access systems and consume data securely.

An organization's Enterprise Security Policy is an integral part of an information security program because it encompasses the human factor of information security. It provides organizations an effective way to educate employees on acceptable system usage, corporate conduct and overall information security. It is one of the first steps in enforcing information security; therefore, it is typically introduced to employees during new hire training. Most organizations require new employees to read and sign an Enterprise Security Policy before they are granted access to any corporate voice or data communication system.

The following example is an Enterprise security policy intended for employees and business partners. It illustrates how a security policy can communicate acceptable system usage while promoting information security. This security policy is intended for informational purposes only.

Enterprise Security Policy

Purpose and Scope

The primary purpose of this Security Policy is to inform employees and non-employees working for or with <Company Name> assets of their shared responsibilities to insure the protection of <Company Name> systems and corporate data. InfoSec is responsible for auditing and maintaining policy compliance. Human Resources is responsible for ensuring that all employees and non-employees working for or with <Company Name> assets have read and signed this Security Policy before they gain access to any <Company Name> voice and data communication systems.

This Security Policy applies to all employees, and non-employees at <Company Name>. This policy applies to all equipment and assets that are owned or leased by <Company Name>.

Responsibilities

All voice and data communication systems and related transmitted information, including but not limited to computer equipment, software, operating systems, storage media, network accounts providing electronic mail, internet browsing and FTP, are the property of <Company Name>. <Company Name> has the right to monitor and review usage of all voice and data communication systems at any time. These systems are to be used for business purposes serving the interests of <Company Name>.

Human Resources

Human Resources' purpose is to provide new hire training, to communicate a security awareness program, and to ensure that all employees and non-employees have read and signed this Security Policy before they gain assess to any <Company Name> systems. This department also ensures that up-to-date policies are easily available to employees.

Management

Management ensures that all personnel have reviewed this policy and are in compliance and are to contact InfoSec immediately if a policy violation is discovered.

InfoSec

InfoSec develops and maintains security policies, identifies and deploys automated security controls and audits for policy compliance.

Employee

An employee should review this policy and all referenced policies herewith to maintain compliance.

Related Policies

Acceptable Use Policy
Password Policy

Scheduled Review

Annually

Security Policy Table of Contents

Physical Security

Physical security is an essential part of <Company Name> information security program. Physical security forms the basis for all other security efforts, including data security. <Company Name> employs physical security controls for its employees and assets. These controls must be followed by all <Company Name> employees.

- Wear your badge at all times while on company property.
- Lock your office door or cubicle storage when you leave your area.
- Lock your computer when stepping away from your work area.
- Log off your workstation at the end of the working day.
- Escort, observe and supervise guests for their entire visit.
- Watch out for "tailgaters." Tailgaters wait for an authorized person to enter a controlled area (such as with a locked door) and then follow him or her through the door.
- Shred or otherwise destroy all sensitive information and media when it is no longer necessary.
- Do not allow anyone to add hardware or software to your computer without proper authorization.
- Do not allow the removal of any corporate assets without ensuring that the person removing it has proper authorization.
- Report suspicious activities to your manager.

Internet Usage

Internet usage is provided as a business service for the purpose of supporting <Company Name> business activities and occasional personal use as defined in the Acceptable Use Policy. Information found on the Internet may not be safe and should be considered suspect until confirmed by a reliable source. All Internet access is monitored and logged.

Messaging systems and Email Access

Corporate email access is provided as a business service for the purpose of supporting <Company Name> business activities as defined in the Acceptable Use Policy. Email is not a secure medium and care should be taken with regard to the information sent in email. Accessing personal email systems like Hotmail, Yahoo, or Gmail is prohibited.

Employees may have access to confidential information about the Company, our employees or clients. With approval of management, employees may use email to communicate confidential information to those with a need to know. Such email must be labeled "Confidential." When in doubt, do not use email to communicate confidential material. All email activity is monitored and logged.

Anti-virus

Viruses, worms and Trojan horses are examples of malware programs that can cause significant damage to <Company Name> data and resources. They can destroy, alter or disclose confidential information in a variety of ways and damage the reputation of <Company Name> as well as the reputation and credibility of <Company Name> employees. <Company Name> employs anti-virus controls for its computers and employees as defined in the Acceptable Use Policy.

These controls must be followed by all <Company Name> employees:
- Ensure that the corporate standard anti-virus software is installed on desktop and laptop computers.
- Employees will not use a computer without anti-virus software on <Company Name's> network, nor will they disable the software.
- Do not open any email attachments from an unknown, suspicious or untrustworthy source. Delete these attachments

immediately. Then "double delete" them by emptying your Trash.

- To avoid spreading a virus, do not create network file shares that allow the 'everyone group' to write to it, unless there is a business reason.
- In the event of a virus, disconnect from the network and contact the Help Desk, InfoSec or your manager immediately.
- Do not download files from questionable sources.

Unauthorized Networks

Wireless technology allows mobile access to <Company Name's> internal network. Only wireless access points and modem connections installed and supported by <Company Name> IT personnel are permitted to connect to <Company Name> network. All other wireless access points and modems that connect to <Company Name> network are prohibited. Employees are prohibited from connecting modems or wireless access points on company property.

Remote Access

Remote Access is provided as a business service for the purpose of supporting <Company Name> business activities as defined in the Acceptable Use Policy. Access for remote users to the corporate network will be from an approved encrypted connection exclusively from corporate managed devices as described in the Acceptable Use Policy. <Company Name> will offer handheld devices for remote access to email.

System Access Passwords

Passwords are an important part of information security and are the primary control used to protect user accounts and sensitive corporate data. Intruders often gain access to a company's systems by stealing or cracking a password and account name and then posing as that user. Intruders often gain access by trying password combinations related to a person's family, address or hobbies. As such, all employees and business partners with access to <Company Name> systems are responsible for selecting a strong password as defined in <Company Name> Password Policy.

Enforcement

Any employee found to have violated any part of this policy may be subject to disciplinary action, up to and including termination of employment.

Employee Acknowledgment

If you have questions or concerns about this policy, contact the Human Resources Department before signing this agreement.

I have read <Company Name's> security policy and agree to abide by it. I understand violation of any of the above terms may result in discipline, up to and including my termination.

Employee Name: (Printed) _____

Employee Signature: _____

Date: _____

Summary

The example Enterprise Security Policy was provided to show how policy is used to reduce risk associated with user access to information systems. An Enterprise Security Policy educates employees and business partners on appropriate system usage and explains the consequences of policy violation. In many cases, this type of policy may be the only security education an employee or business partner receives. Compliance with an Enterprise Security Policy will shore up the overall security posture of the Enterprise and provide a secure foundation for a Terminal Server environment.

Network topographies and infrastructure design play an important role with an Enterprise Architecture. Enterprise Security Architecture introduces Risk Management methodologies along with infrastructure design concepts, such as defense in depth, principle of least privilege, compartmentalization of information, security domains, trust levels and tiered networks. Enterprise Security Architecture design concepts allow organizations to implement the appropriate security controls from an infrastructure design perspective based on the sensitivity and criticality of users, information, applications and business processes.

The next section reviews defense in depth, principle of least privilege, compartmentalization of information and security domains.

Defense in Depth

Defense in Depth (DiD) was originally a military strategy used to delay rather than prevent an attack by using multiple layers of protection. The defense in depth strategy has been widely adopted in non-military applications, such as Enterprise security, by implementing multiple layers of techniques and technologies to secure assets. An example of using defense in depth in IT security is to use administrative and technical security controls, each of which utilizes layers of techniques and technologies to provide security.

One important aspect of defense in depth is a balanced focus on three primary elements:

- People
- Technology
- Operations

The people element of Defense in Depth focuses on the endorsement and understanding of the importance of information security by executive management and the value of an information security program. The technology element of Defense in Depth focuses on the technologies used to meet corporate security requirements. The operations element of Defense in Depth focuses on the processes used to ensure the security of information assets of the organization.

Previous chapters have explained how Enterprise security starts with the commitment of executive management and is followed by the development of policies that define roles, responsibilities and personal accountability. Enterprise Architecture and Enterprise Security Architecture used with a control framework encompass the people, technology and operations element of the defense in depth strategy by providing multiple layers of security techniques and technologies.

Principle of Least Privilege

The principle of least privilege was originally described 30 years ago as a design principle in a paper named "The Protection of Information in Computer Systems" by Jerry Saltzer and Mike Schroeder:

"f) Least privilege: Every program and every user of the system should operate using the least set of privileges necessary to complete the job. Primarily, this principle limits the damage that can result from an accident or error. It also reduces the number of potential interactions among privileged programs to the minimum for correct operation, so that unintentional, unwanted, or improper uses of privilege are less likely to occur. Thus, if a question arises related to misuse of a privilege, the number of programs that must be audited is minimized. Put another way, if a mechanism can provide "firewalls," the principle of least privilege provides a rationale for where to install the firewalls. The military security rule of "need-to-know" is an example of this principle."

In terms of IT security, the principle of least privilege applies to users, applications and systems. Users should be granted the least privilege required to accomplish their jobs.

Applications should be granted the least privilege needed to perform their functions, and systems should be granted the least privilege necessary to fulfill their role in a larger network. The principle of least privilege is important for meeting integrity objectives. In spy and war movies, following the principle of least privilege is equivalent to operating on a "need to know" basis.

Compartmentalization of Information

Compartmentalization of information is actually a subset of the principle of least privilege that focuses on information. Compartmentalization of information limits access to information to people with the "need to know" in order to perform certain tasks. With regard to infrastructure design with Terminal Server, compartmentalization of information is used to compartmentalize users, applications, data and information based on its sensitivity and criticality.

The principle of least privilege and compartmentalization of information are security controls that are used together with infrastructure design and Terminal Server to control access to applications, data and information based on its sensitivity, criticality and value.

Security Domains

Security domains allow organizations to segment their Enterprise network into discrete units. Each security domain will have its own policies that apply security controls based on the sensitivity, criticality and value of the information and systems in a security domain. Policies within the data/information architecture domain, specifically the Data/information Classification and Categorization Policy, can provide guidance to determine the placement of systems, information and data into their respected security domain.

Tip: FIPS PUB 199, which is the "Standards for Security Categorization of Federal Information and Information Systems," provides a formula to determine the security category of systems and can be used to determine within which security domain systems should reside.

Security Domain Classifications:

The classification of security domains is very similar to data classifications. Each infrastructure component will be classified and placed in its respective security domain. The majority of Enterprise networks can be separated into the following four security domains:

- **Controlled**: A controlled security domain is used to restrict access between security domains. A controlled security domain could contain groups of users with their network equipment or a demilitarized zone (DMZ) with a VPN, proxy and web servers.
- **Uncontrolled**: An uncontrolled security domain refers to any network not in control of an organization, such as the Internet.
- **Restricted**: A restricted security domain can represent an organization's production network. Access is restricted to authorized personnel, and there is no direct access from the Internet.

- **Secured**: A secured security domain is a network that is only accessible to a small group of highly trusted users, such as administrators and auditors.

Figure 5.2 shows an Enterprise network divided into four separate security domains.

Figure 5.2

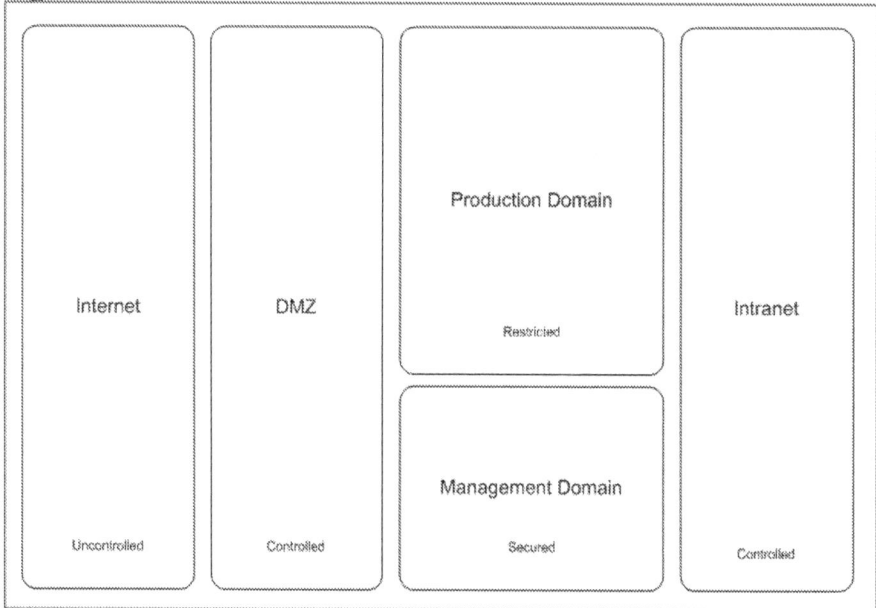

Note: The space between each security domain specifies a firewall that clearly delineates each perimeter from the next.

Example Network Topologies

This section highlights the pros and cons of two network topologies that use the Enterprise Security Architecture design concepts just reviewed. The first example shows a segmented network connected to the Internet with a firewall. The second example differs from the first by using additional segmentation within the controlled and restricted security domains. These examples show how infrastructure design concepts with Terminal Server allow organizations to meet information security and regulatory requirements.

The network topology examples in this chapter do not include all possible situations. There are organizations that extensively segment their networks to meet business objectives and regulatory requirements. However, the design concepts discussed here can be translated to include other architectures and environments.

Example 1

Example 1 shows a segmented network with three security domains connected to the Internet with a firewall. A firewall separates a controlled (DMZ) security domain from a restricted (production) security domain, and a router separates a controlled (intranet) security domain from the restricted security domain. Each security domain is a separate network segment. A firewall and router are used to filter network traffic between security domains.

Figure 5.3 shows Example 1.

Figure 5.3

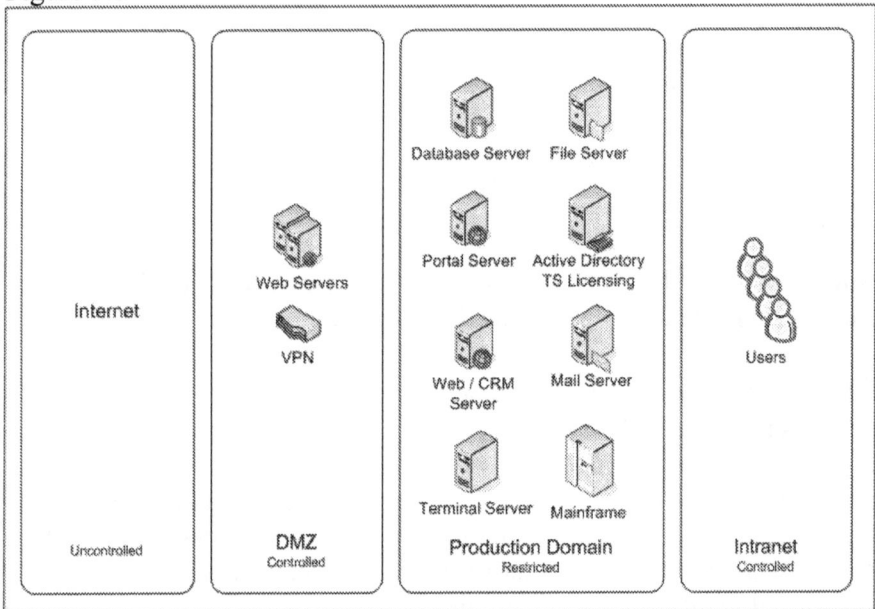

In Example 1, a router is placed between the intranet and production security domain to filter traffic between domains. From a design perspective, there are many considerations with regard to traffic filtering between the intranet and production security domains. We will review two different approaches, one where the router allows a wide variety of traffic between security domains and the other using Terminal Server to limit traffic between security domains to a single port. The latter example illustrates how Terminal Server can be leveraged to reduce the number of open ports between security zones.

In Example 1, users access resources in the production security domain from domain member PCs. This approach requires a wide variety of ports to be open between security domains, allowing PCs to communicate with and receive resources from servers in the production security domain. In the example, services and resources, such as domain authentication, file, print, web, email and Terminal Server, are the services that require communication and open ports between security domains.

Table 5.1 shows the ports and services used in the first example.

Table 5.1

Protocol	Service	Port	Description
TCP	RPC	135	Microsoft's RPC implementation runs over TCP port 135. RPC is used by a number of higher level protocols for their transport layer, such as by DCOM.
UDP	Domain	53	Domain Name Server (DNS). DNS servers offer different services on TCP and UDP. TCP is used for "zone transfers" of full name record databases, while UDP is used for individual lookups. Zone Transfers will provide an entire network map.
TCP	Domain	53	
UDP	Kerberos	88	Kerberos traffic uses UDP/TCP protocol source and destination port 88. It's a default authentication protocol.
TCP	Kerberos	88	
UDP	netbios-ns	137	NetBIOS Name Service (NBNS) is also known as Windows Internet Name Service (WINS).

TCP	netbios-ssn	139	NetBIOS Session Service. The Session Service is used to handle NBT sessions.
TCP	microsoft-ds	445	SMB Direct. Since Windows 2000 Microsoft added the ability to run SMB directly over TCP/IP, without the extra layer of NBT.
TCP	LDAP	389	Lightweight Directory Access Protocol (LDAP), used by Active Directory, Active Directory Connector, and the Microsoft Exchange Server directory.
UDP	LDAP	389	
TCP	LDAP to Global Catalog	3268	LDAP to Global Catalog search communication.
TCP	POP3	110	POP (Post Office Protocol) is used by mail clients to retrieve email.
TCP	HTTP	80	World Wide Web HTTP. Port 80 is the primary port used by the world wide web (www) system.
TCP	HTTPS	443	HTTP protocol over TLS/SSL. This port is used for secure web browser communication.
TCP	RDP	3389	Microsoft Remote Display Protocol. This port is used by Microsoft Terminal Services.

This first example is a common topology in a Windows domain environment in which PCs are domain members, centrally managed by Active Directory and have locally installed client-server applications. This scenario adds risk because of the amount of open ports between the production and intranet security domains, which could be used by viruses, worms or an intruder to compromise systems in either security domain. With this topology, most organizations run similar PC operating systems as their servers. A monolithic operating system approach, together with a wide range of open ports between network segments, introduces the risk that a PC virus or worm that is introduced in one security domain could spread to similar operating systems in other security domains.

The second example as shown in Figure 5.4 uses Terminal Server as the primary application and data access solution. In this scenario, a router is used to filter network traffic between security domains and Terminal Server, which is used to filter and monitor all application and data access. This configuration reduces the amount of open ports between the intranet and production security domains to port "3389" for RDP traffic. Limiting the open ports to 3389 between the intranet and production security domains is an ideal solution in a thin client or unmanaged PC environment because the thin clients or PCs communicate directly with the Terminal Servers on port 3389. All access to applications and data can be rigorously audited from router and Terminal Server logs. Leveraging this configuration with Terminal Server reduces the number of open ports between security domains which reduces the attack surface between security domains. This model is commonly referred to as a data center enclave through which the production security domain classification is secured, not restricted. This model considers the intranet security domain as uncontrolled and treats all user access as remote access, similar to an Application Service Provider (ASP) or Software as a Service (SAAS) model.

Typically, organizations use a configuration somewhere in the middle of these the two examples. They support managed domain member PCs in the intranet security domain with the minimum number open ports between security domains to meet business requirements. Organizations that adopt a thin client model are able to limit traffic between the intranet and production domain to 3389 effectively, creating a data center enclave.

Let's shift focus from the router configurations between the intranet and production security domains and look at the overall design with regard to defense in depth, compartmentalization of information and network segmentation. The first example shows a segmented network with three security domains connected to the Internet with a firewall. From an infrastructure design perspective, the defense in depth strategy is implemented by using network segmentation. Network segmentation provides multiple layers of defense from a networking perspective, such as traffic filtering between security domains. With the addition of administrative and technical security controls, such as encryption, virus prevention and operating system hardening, defense in depth is demonstrated with multiple layers of security.

In terms of compartmentalization of information, the first example highlights design deficiencies to effectively compartmentalize users, applications, data, and information based on their sensitivity, criticality, and value within a security domain. A design deficiency exists when a necessary control is missing or an existing control is not properly designed. A security breach or virus outbreak on any system in the intranet or production security domains will be challenging to isolate from other systems on the same network segment. For example, if a server in the production security domains is compromised, it could be used as a hacking vector to other machines on the same network.

In terms of infrastructure designs, the first example requires additional segmentation within the intranet and production security domains in order to provide compartmentalization of information. The lack of segmentation within the intranet and production security domains can be of particular concern for organizations with must comply with regulatory mandates like Sarbanes-Oxley, Health Insurance Portability and Accountability and Gramm-Leach-Bliley.

Example 2

Example 2 differs from the first by using additional segmentation within the intranet and production security domains. This strategy allows compartmentalization of users, applications and data based on their sensitivity, criticality and value within a security domain. Each segment is on a separate isolated network and governed by its own policies that describe the security requirements of the isolated network. If a security breach or virus outbreaks on a system in one segment occurs, it could be isolated within its security domain. Network segmentation is accomplished by using a firewall, router or VLAN to partition, control and monitor traffic between security domains.

Figure 5.4 shows Example 2. Each security domain is a separate network segment. A firewall and router are used to filter network traffic between security domains.

Figure 5.4

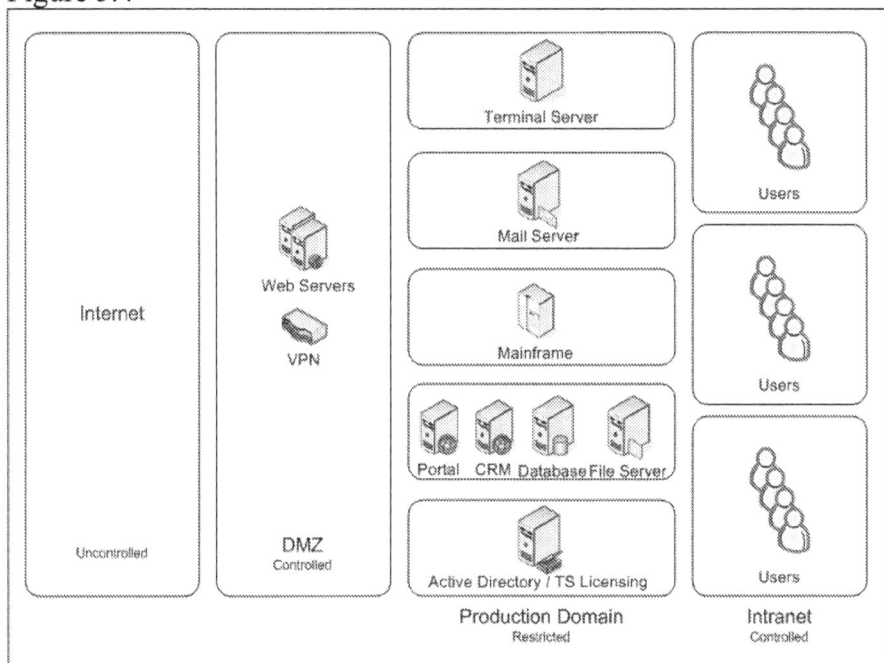

Figure 5.4 shows the intranet security domain with three isolated segments. One segment is dedicated for the general office productivity population, the second for developers, and a third for the finance department. This strategy supports compartmentalization of information. For example, if a security incident such as a virus occurs in the general office productivity population, it would be easier to isolate within its security domain.

The production security domain has five isolated segments, and each segment is a separate isolated network. It contains a dedicated segment for the Terminal Servers, email, mainframe, directory services, and one for web, database and file server. Segmentation allows for compartmentalization of resources along with the configuration of granular traffic and filtering rules between segments and security domains. The design strategy shown in Figure 5.4 allows the implementation of the appropriate security control such as encryption or logging to segments and security domains based on their sensitivity, criticality and value.

Chapter 5 Summary

This chapter discussed Enterprise Security Architecture and introduced an example Risk Assessment Policy and Enterprise Security Policy. The chapter concluded with Enterprise Security Architecture infrastructure design concepts.

Enterprise Security Architecture

- Enterprise Security Architecture introduces Risk Management techniques, methodologies and practices.
- Enterprise Architecture provides the foundation to develop and deploy technologies while Enterprise Security Architecture is used as a guideline in making strategic, architectural security decisions.
- Defense in Depth (DiD) was originally a military strategy used to delay rather than prevent an attack by using multiple layers of protection.
- The principle of least privilege applies to users, applications and systems. Users should be granted the least privilege required to accomplish their jobs. Applications should be granted the least privilege to perform their functions, and systems should be granted the least privilege to fulfill their role in a larger network.
- Compartmentalization of information limits access to information to those people with the "need to know" in order to perform certain tasks.
- In regards to infrastructure design with Terminal Server, compartmentalization of information is used to compartmentalize users, applications, data and information based on its sensitivity and criticality.
- Security domains allow organizations to segment their Enterprise network into discrete units. Each security domain will have its own policies that apply security controls based on the sensitivity, criticality and value of the information and systems in a security domain.

The next chapter will provide an overview of physical and environmental security. Chapter 6 will explain the necessity of physical security in terms of protecting the confidentiality, integrity, and availability of an organization's assets.

Resources:
The SANS Policy Project
Enclave STIG, V3R1
NSA Defense in Depth
http://www.nsa.gov/snac/support/defenseindepth.pdf#search=%22Def
ense%20in%20Depth%22
Needed: an Enterprise Security Architecture
http://www.networkworld.com/columnists/2006/050806minoli.html?prl
The Protection of Information in Computer Systems from Saltzer and Schroeder
http://www.cs.virginia.edu/~evans/cs551/saltzer/

Chapter 6: Physical and Environmental Security

Chapter Overview:
This chapter introduces physical and environmental security. As discussed in Chapter 4, an Enterprise Architecture provides policies that encompass physical and environmental security. Chapter 6 builds on what we learned from previous chapters by providing a brief explanation of physical and environmental security as an introduction to the physical and environmental security controls used to protect a Terminal Server environment. The discussion evolves to physical and environmental security in terms of Terminal Server and regulatory compliance by introducing an example tier 2 IT Server Room Policy. Chapter 6 illustrates the importance of physical and environmental security, provides additional references, and explains why systems must be protected in a secure location against unauthorized access, environmental threats and manmade disasters.

The overwhelming consensuses in all walks of security professionals is that if an attacker gains physical access to an environment, all existing security controls are pointless. Once an organization's physical security has been compromised, even the most hardened server is at risk to a variety of threats.

Physical and environmental security is not the most popular topic of discussion among IT professionals because the controls rarely involve the hardware, software and firmware technologists support. The NIST Special Publication 800-33 describes physical security as a "non-computing security method."

Physical and environmental security addresses the threats, vulnerabilities and countermeasures used to secure an organization's assets. Physical and environmental security encompasses people, facilities, data, equipment, media and supplies. Physical and environmental security includes administrative controls, physical access controls and environmental protection controls. An example of administrative controls is visitor registration. Physical access controls can be as simple as a locked door or as elaborate as biometric access controls behind multiple guard posts. Environmental protection can be as simple as surge protection and a fire extinguisher or as elaborate as full scale climate control, conditioned power or emergency power sources with an automated fire protection system. In terms of Terminal Server, physical and environmental security provides the security controls that ensure against unauthorized access, environmental threats and manmade disasters.

Table 6.1 introduces physical access controls and environmental protection considerations.

Table 6.1

Physical Access Controls	Environmental Protection
Guards	Power Protection and Conditioning
Fences	HVAC
Barriers	Water Protection
Lighting	Fire Detection
Keys and Locks	Fire Suppression
Badges	Evacuation
Escorts	Environmental Monitoring
Monitoring and Detection Systems	Environmental Detection

Organizations that must comply with regulatory mandates, such as Sarbanes-Oxley, Health Insurance Portability, and so forth, must undergo regular audits to ensure compliance. There are a number of widely adopted control frameworks and guidelines that can be used to help implement and audit physical and environmental security.

Table 6.2 lists additional resources.

Table 6.2

Name	Explanation	Section
FIPS PUB 31	U.S. Department of Commerce / National Bureau of Standards, Federal Information Processing Standards (FIPS) Guidelines for automatic data processing physical security and Risk Management. This document is outdated, although it is still considered a good informational resource.	Entire document is dedicated to physical and environmental security.
ISO IEC 17799 2005	The purpose of ISO/IEC 17799 is to provide recommendations for information security management to those responsible for initiating, implementing or maintaining security in their organization.	Section 9.
NIST Special Publication 800-12	An Introduction to Computer Security: The NIST Handbook	Chapter 15.
CobIT 4.0	CobIT is a framework for information IT management risks, or more formally, a "framework and supporting toolset that allows managers to bridge the gap between control requirements, technical issues and business risks" (ref: ISACA). CobIT is typically associated with Sarbanes-Oxley compliance.	• PO4.8 Responsibility for Risk, Security and Compliance. • DS12 Manage the Physical Environment. • DS12.2 Physical Security Measures.

After physical and environmental security has been compromised, even the most hardened server is at risk to a wide range of threats, such as theft, tampering, accidental interference, lose of power, surges or spikes, flood, fire, earthquake, overheating, and so forth. From a server perspective, as soon as physical security is compromised, theft or tampering is a serious concern. Many popular tools are available on the Internet that can be used to reset the local or domain administrator's password by booting a server from a floppy or CDROM. Once an intruder has the administrator's password, it is possible to install root kits or roam the network with immunity. An example of environmental risks includes power irregularities or failure, heat, floods, fire, earthquake, and so forth.

The following example is an IT server Room Security Policy which highlights the security controls employed to protect a server room against unauthorized access, environmental threats and manmade disasters. This policy is intended for informational purposes only.

IT Server Room Security Policy

Purpose and Scope
The purpose of this policy is to ensure that a minimum level of physical and environmental security is maintained in IT Server Rooms. The following policy is applicable to all of <Company Name> IT Server Rooms, employees and visitors who access any IT Server Rooms.

Roles and Responsibilities

Director of IT
In order to ensure compliance with this policy, the Director of IT is responsible for distributing this policy to all employees who access IT server rooms.

All Employees
All employees shall read this policy before accessing IT server rooms. It is the responsibility of <Company Name> employees to ensure that

they carry out their duties in a professional manner while working in IT Server Rooms.

Visitors

All visitors shall be accompanied by a member of the IT staff at all times while in an IT server room. It is the responsibility of the <Company Name> IT staff accompanying the visitor to ensure they carry out their duties in a professional manner while working in IT Server Rooms.

Policy

- The primary security control used to access the IT server rooms is a digital door lock.
- Only authorized personnel shall be allowed access to the server room area, including those persons needed to operate, supervise or provide maintenance to the area and its equipment.
- Personnel shall wear their identification badge at all times while in an IT server room.
- All visitors must wear visitors' passes while in an IT server room.
- All visitors must be accompanied by <Company Name> IT staff at all times while in an IT server room.
- Tailgating other staff members in order to enter an IT server room is not permitted.
- Food and drink shall not be taken into the IT server rooms.
- The server room must have clean, conditioned power.
- A primary and back-up uninterrupted power system (UPS) is required to prevent data loss if the main power should fail.
- The server room must have a primary and backup climate control system.
- Database and file backups will be kept as current as is reasonable. All backup tapes must be stored in a secured off-site location.

Policy Review

This policy will be reviewed annually.

Compliance
Any employee found to have violated this policy may be subject to disciplinary action, up to and including termination of employment.

Reference
FIPS PUB 31
ISO IEC 17799 2005
NIST Special Publication 800-12
NIST Handbook Chapter 15

The proceeding policy shows which security controls organizations employ to protect their information systems including Terminal Server from unauthorized access, environmental threats and manmade disasters.

Chapter 6 Summary
This chapter discussed physical and environmental security and provided an example tier 2 IT Server Room Policy.

- If an attacker gains physical access to an environment, all existing security controls are pointless.
- Physical and environmental security addresses the threats, vulnerabilities and countermeasures used to secure an organization's assets.
- Physical and environmental security encompasses people, facilities, data, equipment, media and supplies.
- Physical access controls can be as simple as a locked door or as elaborate as biometric access controls behind multiple guard posts.
- Organizations that must comply with regulatory mandates, like Sarbanes-Oxley, Health Insurance Portability, and others, must undergo regular audits to ensure compliance.

The next chapter will review password security and a sample tier 2 Password Policy that defines a standard for creation of strong passwords, the protection of those passwords and the frequency of change.

Resources
FIPS PUB 31
ISO IEC 17799 2005
NIST Special Publication 800-12
NIST Handbook Chapter 15
Cobit PO4.8 Responsibility for Risk, Security and Compliance
Cobit DS12 Manage the Physical Environment
Cobit DS12.2 Physical Security Measures

.

Chapter 7: Password Policy

Chapter Overview:
This chapter will review password security and introduce a Password Policy. This chapter builds on the Enterprise Security Policy from Chapter 5, which referenced a Password Policy in the System Access Passwords section. We will review how a Password Policy fits within an Enterprise Architecture, the importance of password security, an overview of password cracking and conclude with an example Password Policy.

A Password Policy is an administrative security control that works together with other Enterprise Architecture security controls to provide layered security through the Enterprise. For example in Chapter 5, the Enterprise Security Policy defined how organizations educate their employees and business partners on approved system and data usage. The example Enterprise Security Policy in Chapter 5 referenced a Password Policy and an Acceptable Use Policy. Together these policies reduce risk by implementing layered security controls (defense in depth) through the Enterprise. A Password Policy is an important security control that provides front line security to an organization's network because a poorly chosen password can result in the breach of its network and assets. Organizations that must comply with regulatory mandates, such as with classified information, a password policy violation could be considered a criminal offense.

Weak password security in a Terminal Server environment poses additional risk because anyone internally or externally with network access to a Terminal Server can display a Windows logon screen. The ability to display a Windows logon screen makes weak passwords and password cracking especially worrisome. If an intruder can view a Windows logon screen, password cracking software can be executed against user accounts or administrator accounts, the latter by design does not have an account lockout policy.

As discussed in Chapter 5, passwords are a very important part of information security and are an instrumental administrative security control used to protect user accounts and corporate assets. Intruders often gain access to systems by stealing or cracking a password and account name and then posing as that user. As such, all employees and business partners with access to an organization's systems will follow the steps outlined in a Password Policy to select and secure their passwords.

Password Policies define password length, password construction, password duration, password hygiene and password compliance. Password length defines the minimum password length. Password construction defines the requirements on selecting a password to include the criteria in selecting a strong password that is hard to guess but easy to remember. Password duration defines how often a password is changed. Passwords can be changed at each logon, monthly, quarterly, or at other intervals, depending on the criticality of the information needing protection and the frequency with which a password is used. The more times a password is used, the more chance there is of it being compromised. Password hygiene defines the use and management of passwords. An example of password hygiene would be not sharing a password or not saving a password on a piece of paper. Password compliance defines disciplinary actions for users that do not comply with the Password Policy.

List 7.1 shows common password vulnerabilities:
- User accounts with weak or non-existent passwords.
- Automatically generated accounts by operating systems and applications with weak or non-existent passwords.
- In spite of the strength of a user's password, users fail to protect it and write it down on a piece of paper that is commonly found near their PC.
- Many commercial and Open Source applications use known hashing algorithms. All too often these hashes are stored where users can access and compromise them.

The point here is that mitigating weak passwords is one of the first steps to enhance the security posture of a network. Implementing a strong password policy is a necessary step in securing the Enterprise.

Password cracking is the technical method of recovering lost or unknown passwords that are stored on computers. A password cracker is an application that is used by administrators and hackers to guess unknown or forgotten passwords. Administrators generally use and, in many cases, automate password crackers to test for password compliance; in contrast, hackers try to gain user or root level access to a machine.

Most password cracking software focus on guessing passwords, not decrypting encrypted passwords. This approach is used because most contemporary encryption algorithms are one-way as there is no reverse process that will reveal a password in plain text. So guessing a password using a brute force or dictionary attack (explained below) is more efficient than trying to decrypt a password. Incidentally, the only way for an organization to audit password compliance is to test each and every user name and password by using a password cracking application. Most organizations sanction regular password compliance auditing, which explicitly permits auditing password complexity in order to check for passwords that are easily compromised and, when appropriate, help users recover forgotten passwords.

Please Note: Never run password recovery tools without explicit and preferably written permission from your employer or customer. Network and security administrators with the best intentions have been terminated for running password recovery tools without proper authority to do so.

The term password cracking is synonymous with password recovery. Over the years password cracking has transformed into a commercial password recovery market. A fantastic example of this transformation is the widely distributed, award-winning NT password cracking application L0phtCrack, which was originally developed by L0pht Heavy Industries. L0pht Heavy Industries was a hackers' think tank founded in the early 1990s that merged in January 2000 with a startup computer security company named @stake. From a media standpoint, the merger was positioned as a transition of L0pht Heavy Industries, considered by the media as an illicit black hat group of hackers, to a licit white hat security company. Symantec announced its acquisition of @stake on September 16, 2004, and today L0phtCrack is a Symantec password recovery product sold under the name of @stake LC 5.

There are primarily two methods of password cracking: (i) social engineering, and (ii) password cracking. Social engineering means manipulating people to provide their user names and passwords. Password cracking uses software to automatically generate passwords in order to gain unauthorized access to computer systems. In the book *The Art of Deception,* Kevin Mitnick astutely notes that it is simply easier to trick a user into giving you his or her user name and password than expending time and computing resources performing password cracking! This statement emphasizes the importance of security awareness training and a Password Policy.

Tip: I would like to encourage you pick up *The Art of Deception*, and read it; and if necessary, reassess your organization's security procedures accordingly.

Password crackers primary use two methods to identify correct passwords: brute-force and dictionary attacks. A brute force attack enters every possible combination of characters and numbers until the machine accepts one of the combinations as the correct password. A dictionary attack enters each word in the dictionary to guess the correct password. Most password crackers can search a hybrid of dictionary entries and numbers by using a variety of methods including parsing a file to help add numbers to the characters of a search. The ability to search a hybrid of dictionary entries and numbers can be very useful with corporations that require their users to include a number in their password. Despite the known risk of password attacks, user accounts with simple to guess or empty passwords remain exceptionally common, and good password policies are unfortunately far too rare, as is the enforcement of a password policy when one exists.

With password cracking, a goal of many hackers is to get the local or domain administrator account password on any machine they are able to access. Once hackers have an administrator's password, they have the proverbial keys to the kingdom and, in most cases, can gain access to just about any other machine or device on the network. Passwords discovered on one machine frequently are reused on other machines, allowing an attacker to roam about with impunity with the appearance of being a legitimate corporate user. One of the common denominators of password cracking is that an attacker presumably already has some degree of access to the target machine or network, such as an employee, consultant or business partner.

List 7.2 shows the type of attacks that can provide an attacker with multiple passwords to authenticate to a system:
- Password sniffing
- Brute-force or dictionary attack against an encrypted password file
- Dumpster diving
- Social engineering

All of the above attacks can help an intruder find passwords to access systems, but a dictionary attack on an encrypted password file would more likely provide an attacker with multiple passwords that could be used to access other accounts and systems. Password sniffing can only provide an intruder with some encrypted passwords, provided that they can sniff the packets during a logon event. Dumpster diving consists largely of rummaging about through other's trash looking for useful things that could provide a dumpster diver with user name and passwords if they are not properly protected.

The following is an example Password Policy from the SANS Security Policy Project. It starts with an overview section, purpose and scope and then delivers the password policy. This policy is intended for informational purposes only.

Password Policy

Overview
Passwords are an important aspect of computer security. They are the front line of protection for user accounts. A poorly chosen password

may result in the compromise of <Company Name> entire corporate network. As such, all <Company Name> employees (including contractors and vendors with access to <Company Name> systems) are responsible for taking the appropriate steps, as outlined below, to select and secure their passwords.

Purpose
The purpose of this policy is to establish a standard for the creation of strong passwords, the protection of those passwords and the frequency of change.

Scope
The scope of this policy includes all personnel who have or are responsible for an account (or any form of access that supports or requires a password) on any system that resides at any <Company Name> facility, has access to the <Company Name> network, or stores any non-public <Company Name> information.

Policy
General
- All system-level passwords (e.g., root, enable, NT admin, application administration accounts, etc.) must be changed on at least a quarterly basis.
- All production system-level passwords must be part of the InfoSec administered global password management database.
- All user-level passwords (e.g., email, web, desktop computer, etc.) must be changed at least every six months. The recommended change interval is every four months.
- User accounts that have system-level privileges granted through group memberships must have a unique password from all other accounts held by that user.
- Passwords must not be inserted into email messages or other forms of electronic communication.
- Where SNMP is used, the community strings must be defined as something other than the standard defaults of "public", "private" and "system" and must be different from the passwords used to log in interactively. A keyed hash must be used where available (e.g., SNMPv2).

- All user-level and system-level passwords must conform to the guidelines described below.

Guidelines
A. General Password Construction Guidelines
Passwords are used for various purposes at <Company Name>. Some of the more common uses include: user level accounts, web accounts, email accounts, screen saver protection, voicemail password and local router logins. Since very few systems have support for one-time tokens, (i.e., dynamic passwords which are only used once), everyone should be aware of how to select strong passwords.

Poor, weak passwords have the following characteristics:

- The password contains less than eight characters.
- The password is a word found in a dictionary (English or foreign.)
- The password is a common usage word such as:
  - Names of family, pets, friends, co-workers, fantasy characters, etc.
  - Computer terms and names, commands, sites, companies, hardware, software.
  - The words "<Company Name>", "sanjose", "sanfran" or any derivation.
  - Birthdays and other personal information such as addresses and phone numbers.
  - Word or number patterns like aaabbb, qwerty, zyxwvuts, 123321, etc.
  - Any of the above spelled backwards.
  - Any of the above preceded or followed by a digit (e.g., secret1, 1secret.)

Strong passwords have the following characteristics:

- Contain both upper and lower case characters (e.g., a-z, A-Z)
- Have digits and punctuation characters as well as letters e.g., 0-9, !@#$%^&*()_+|~-=\`{}[]:";'<>?,./)
- Are at least eight alphanumeric characters long.
- Are not a word in any language, slang, dialect, jargon, etc.

o Are not based on personal information, names of family, etc.
o Passwords should never be written down or stored on-line. Try to create passwords that can be easily remembered. One way to do this is create a password based on a song title, affirmation or other phrase. For example, the phrase might be: "This May Be One Way to Remember" and the password could be: "TmB1w2R!" or "Tmb1W>r~" or some other variation.

NOTE: Do not use either of these examples as passwords!

B. Password Protection Standards

Do not use the same password for <Company Name> accounts as for other non-<Company Name> access (e.g., personal ISP account, option trading, benefits, etc.). Where possible, don't use the same password for various <Company Name> access needs. For example, select one password for the Engineering systems and a separate password for IT systems. Also, select a separate password to be used for an NT account and a UNIX account.

Do not share <Company Name> passwords with anyone, including administrative assistants or secretaries. All passwords are to be treated as sensitive, confidential <Company Name> information.

Here is a list of "don'ts":

o Don't reveal a password over the phone to ANYONE.
o Don't reveal a password in an email message.
o Don't reveal a password to the boss.
o Don't talk about a password in front of others.
o Don't hint at the format of a password (e.g., "my family name".)
o Don't reveal a password on questionnaires or security forms.
o Don't share a password with family members.
o Don't reveal a password to co-workers while on vacation.

If someone demands a password, refer them to this document or have them call someone in the Information Security Department.

Do not use the "Remember Password" feature of applications (e.g., Eudora, Outlook, Netscape Messenger).

Again, do not write passwords down and store them anywhere in your office. Do not store passwords in a file on ANY computer system (including Palm Pilots or similar devices) without encryption.

Change passwords at least once every six months (except system-level passwords which must be changed quarterly). The recommended change interval is every four months.

If an account or password is suspected to have been compromised, report the incident to InfoSec and change all passwords.

Password cracking or guessing may be performed on a periodic or random basis by InfoSec or its delegates. If a password is guessed or cracked during one of these scans, the user will be required to change it.

C. Application Development Standards
Application developers must ensure their programs contain the following security precautions. Applications:
o Should support authentication of individual users, not groups.
o Should not store passwords in clear text or in any easily reversible form.
o Should provide for some sort of role management, such that one user can take over the functions of another without having to know the other's password.
o Should support TACACS+, RADIUS and/or X.509 with LDAP security retrieval, wherever possible.

D. Use of Passwords and Passphrases for Remote Access Users
Access to the <Company Name> Networks via remote access is to be controlled using either a one-time password authentication or a public/private key system with a strong passphrase.

E. Passphrases
Passphrases are generally used for public/private key authentication. A public/private key system defines a mathematical relationship between the public key that is known by all, and the private key, that is known

only to the user. Without the passphrase to "unlock" the private key, the user cannot gain access.

Passphrases are not the same as passwords. A passphrase is a longer version of a password and is, therefore, more secure. A passphrase is typically composed of multiple words. Because of this, a passphrase is more secure against "dictionary attacks."

A good passphrase is relatively long and contains a combination of upper and lowercase letters and numeric and punctuation characters. An example of a good passphrase:

"The*?#>*@TrafficOnThe101Was*&#!#ThisMorning"

All of the rules above that apply to passwords apply to passphrase.

Compliance
Any employee found to have violated this policy may be subject to disciplinary action, up to and including termination of employment.

Chapter 7 Summary
This chapter introduced password security, highlighted password security in a Terminal Server environment and concluded with an example Password Policy.

- A Password Policy is a critical security control that provides front line security to an organization's network.
- Password Policies define password length, password construction, password duration, password hygiene and password compliance.
- Password security in a Terminal Server environment poses additional risk because anyone with network access to a Terminal Server can display a Windows logon screen.
- Intruders often gain access to systems by stealing or cracking a password and account name and then posing as that user.
- Password cracking consists primarily of two methods: (i) social engineering and (ii) password cracking.

- Most organizations sanction regular password compliance auditing, which explicitly permits auditing password complexity in order to check for easily crackable passwords.
- With password cracking, a goal of many hackers is to get the local or domain administrator account password on any machine they are able to access.
- A key point of password cracking is that an attacker presumably already has some degree of access to the target machine or network, such as an employee, consultant or business partner.

The next chapter will review a sample tier 3 Terminal Server Standards policy that is used to define Enterprise wide Terminal Server standards.

Resources
The SANS Security Policy Project
FIPS PUB 112
Sample Generic Policy and High Level Procedures for Passwords and Access Forms
http://go.microsoft.com/fwlink/?LinkId=22206

Chapter 8: Windows Terminal Server Standards

Chapter Overview:
This chapter introduces an example tier 3 Terminal Server Standards policy that specifies Enterprise wide Terminal Server standards. A Windows Terminal Server Standards policy explicitly states Enterprise wide requirements from a plan, build, run and monitor perspective. It provides personnel with an approved framework to design, implement and support a Windows Terminal Server environment.

Standards are used to provide the uniform use of technologies to drive consistency and reproducibility, lower operational costs, and enable faster deployments of technologies and functions. Standards allow organizations to meet strategic and tactical Information Technology objectives better while maximizing the business value of information technology.

From a security perspective, Windows Terminal Server Standards provide uniformity and predictability which improves the security posture of an environment. The example Terminal Server Standards policy will reference other policies.

The following example is a Windows Terminal Server Standards policy. This policy is intended for informational purposes only.

Windows Terminal Server Standards

Purpose
The purpose of these standards is to define Enterprise wide Windows Terminal Server architecture requirements in order to provide opportunities to meet strategic and tactical Information Technology objectives better. These standards define a template and a set of

requirements used to implement and support Windows Terminal Server.

Scope

These standards are applicable for <Company Name> and any <Company Name> business units that support Windows Terminal Server.

Standards

Terminal Server Architecture and Server Farm Design

Multiple load-balanced Terminal Servers are referred to as a Terminal Server farm which consists of a network load-balancing solution, two or more Terminal Servers and optionally a Session Directory server. A Terminal Server farm allows an organization to scale out its Terminal Server environment by adding servers to the server farm to increase capacity and to scale horizontally.

From a network design perspective, Terminal Servers will be placed within close physical proximity to the data to ensure that as little data as possible traverses over a network, thereby promoting efficiencies in bandwidth management and bandwidth usage.

- A centralized server farm will be established and collocated with application and user data.
- If the data or application cannot be hosted in the centralized data center, a separate Terminal Server or Terminal Server farm will be established within close physical proximity to the data or application.
- When more than two Terminal Servers are deployed, a server farm will be established with a Session Directory and the Microsoft load-balancing service.

Session Directory

- A Session Directory will be installed on a dedicated and highly available server.

Load-Balancing

- The Microsoft load-balancing service will be used.
- All load-balanced farm servers will be on the same subnet.

Terminal Server Licensing Server
- Terminal Server licensing shall be installed on two domain controllers in Enterprise license server mode.

Licensing
- One "server license" for each Terminal Server is required.
- One Terminal Server Client Access License (TSCAL) is required for each user or device that connects to the Terminal Server farm.
- Terminal Server will be configured in per user licensing mode.

Hardware
- 64-bit platform will be used to mitigate the 4GB memory limitations.

CPU
- 2 physical dual-core processors.

Memory
- 12 GB memory.

Hard Disk
- The operating system files and paging files should be placed on separate partitions.
- The system partition should be mirrored, so that in the event of a hard disk failure, users are not disconnected from their sessions.
- The partitions that are to contain the applications shall be configured with a RAID 5 array to ensure that applications remain usable in the event of a single hard disk failure.

Operating System Installation and Configuration

Operating System
- Windows Server 2003 Standard x64 Edition shall be used for single server environment.

- Windows Server 2003 Enterprise x64 Edition shall be used for each member server in a server farm.

Installation

- An automated server build process will be established to maintain consistency and stability and to enable rapid deployment and recovery.

Anti-virus Prevention

- All Terminal Servers will have <Product Name> anti-virus software installed and automated to run at regular intervals.
- Anti-virus software and virus pattern files must be kept up to date.
- Guidelines from the Desktop Application Security Technical Implementation Guide v 3, release 0, Appendix B. Anti-virus Product Specific Guidance will be used to configure and support <Product Name> anti-virus software.

Patch management

- Patch management will be automated using Windows Server Update Services.

Server Security

- All Terminal Servers will comply with <Company Name> Windows Server Security Policy and Terminal Server Security Baseline.

Terminal Server Installation

- All Terminal Servers will comply with <Company Name> Terminal Server Installation Baseline.

Terminal Server Management

- Terminal Servers will be managed in a separate Organizational Unit (OU) by Group Policy.

Securing Terminal Server Sessions

- All Terminal Servers will comply with <Company Name>'s Terminal Server Security Baseline.

Applications

- All applications on Terminal Servers will comply with <Company Name>'s Terminal Server Application Software Policy.

Application Access Rights

- All applications that access classified, financial or human resources data will require access restrictions.

Client Devices

- Client devices that connect to Terminal Servers shall comply with <Company Name>'s Platform Architecture Policy.

RDC Clients

- The Remote Desktop Connection (RDC) client and Remote Desktop Web Connection clients will be supported.

Printing

- Server printers and client printers will be supported.

User Profiles

- Terminal Server roaming user profiles will be implemented.
- User profiles will be managed via Group Policy.
- User profiles will be kept as small as possible.
- Profile size will be limited per Group Policy.
- Creation of new profiles will be fully automated.
- User profiles will be backed up as part of the daily data backup process.

Monitoring and Reporting

- Microsoft Operations Manager (MOM) is the standard monitoring and reporting solution.

Security Policy Auditing

- Security auditing will comply with <Company Name>'s Audit Vulnerability Scan Policy

Incident Response

- All security incidents shall comply with <Company Name>'s Incident Response Policy.

Change Management

- All modifications made to a production Terminal Server shall comply with <Company Name>'s Change Management Policy.

Backups

<Company Name> employs automated server builds, application packaging, and deployment for Terminal Servers with remote storage of all Terminal Server user and application data.

- Terminal Servers will not be backed up.
- Terminal Server roaming profiles will be backed up as part of the daily data backup process.

Review Cycle

- This document will be reviewed annually unless an exception is needed.

Compliance

Any employee found to have violated this policy may be subject to disciplinary action, up to and including termination of employment.

Resources

- Windows Server Security Policy
- Terminal Server Security Baseline
- Terminal Server Application Software Policy
- Audit Vulnerability Scan Policy
- Incident Response Policy
- Platform Architecture Policy
- Desktop Application Security Technical Implementation Guide v 3, release 0, Appendix B. Anti-virus Product Specific Guidance

Chapter 8 Summary

This chapter reviewed an example tier 3 Terminal Server Standards policy. The policy defines Enterprise wide Terminal Server standards and requirements from a plan, build, run and monitor perspective.

- Standards are used to provide a uniform use of a technology that drives consistency and reproducibility, lower operational costs, and enable faster role outs of technologies and functions.
- From a security perspective, a Windows Terminal Server Standards policy provides uniformity and predictability.

These policies and guidelines were referenced within the Terminal Server Standards:
- Windows Server Security Policy
- Terminal Server Security Baseline
- Terminal Server Application Software Policy
- Server Security Auditing Policy
- Incident Response Policy
- Platform Architecture Policy
- Server Monitoring and Reporting Policy
- Desktop Application Security Technical Implementation Guide v 3, release 0, Appendix B. Anti-virus Product Specific Guidance

The next chapter will review a tier 3 Windows Server Security Policy.

Resources:
http://www.microsoft.com/windowsserver2003/techinfo/overview/lock down.mspx

Chapter 9: Windows Server Security Policy

Chapter Overview:
This chapter introduces a tier 3 Windows Server Security Policy that defines an organization's Windows server security and minimum server standards. The implementation of a Windows Server Security Policy improves the security posture of a Windows server environment while satisfying regulatory mandates. Security is improved by implementing the policy's minimum security standards, which are used by employees as a baseline security configuration for all Windows servers. A baseline security configuration can be audited for compliance and easily modified to meet evolving business and regulatory needs.

Windows operating system security is a critical element in securing Terminal Server which is a Windows service that relies on the security of the underlying Windows operating system. Windows server and desktop operating systems have integrated operating system and networking functions. This architecture provides a wide variety of security configurations to secure both the operating system and networking functions. A properly secured Windows server operating system and integrated networking functions provide a secure foundation for Terminal Server.

Many organizations develop, test and support a single generic server build which becomes a baseline for all of their servers. This strategy with a Windows Server Security Policy provides a high level of assurance that all newly provisioned servers meet minimum security standards. As new servers are provisioned and their respected roles, such as Terminal Server, web server, mail server, and so forth, are configured, policy will govern the configuration and management of each individual server role.

The following example Windows Server Security Policy defines an organization's Windows server security and minimum server standards. This policy is intended for informational purposes only.

Windows Server Security Policy

Purpose
The purpose of this policy is to define standards for the baseline configuration of <Company Name>'s Windows servers. Before any servers are placed on the production network, standard processes shall be executed to ensure that the servers are installed and maintained in a manner that prevents unauthorized access, unauthorized use and disruptions in service.

Scope
This policy is specifically for all Windows servers on the internal network and will be reviewed in conjunction with the other IT infrastructure policies.

Policy

General Guidelines
- The operating system installation media will come from an approved source.
- All production servers will be located in a secure facility.
- Server role configurations are governed by the <Server Role Name> Security Baseline.
- All servers deployed into production will be registered in the asset management system. The machine name, server role, operating system, IP address, physical location (building/room) and name of contact person will be included.
- Before any server is put into production, a baseline will be taken in accordance with the Security Technical Implementation Guides (STIGS) WINDOWS 2003/XP/2000 ADDENDUM Version 5, Release 1, Section 2.1. The baseline will be attached to the server's properties in the asset management system.

- When a server is decommissioned, it must be properly sanitized in compliance with the Media Disposal Policy.
- Any server identified as compromised will be subject to the practices of the IT Intrusion Response Plan.
- Logon banners will be displayed before any user signs on to a server as described in Appendix C.

Windows Server Configuration Guidelines
- The local administrator account will be renamed.
- Guest Accounts will be disabled.
- All unnecessary Windows services will be disabled.
- All unnecessary network services will be disabled.
- Screensaver password will be set.
- Audit logging will be enabled via Group Policy.
- Log properties will be configured in accordance with <Company Name>'s Log Configuration Standards.
- Virus software will be installed and updated.

Patch Update Guidelines
- All patches will be tested in the lab environment before they are deployed on production systems.
- High-priority updates will be applied as needed in accordance with <Company Name>'s Change Management Policy.
- Non-critical fixes will be applied on a Quarterly basis in accordance with <Company Name>'s Change Management Policy.

File System Guidelines
- All servers will be configured in accordance with the Security Technical Implementation Guides (STIGS) WINDOWS 2003/XP/2000 ADDENDUM Version 5, Release 1, Section 7.1 and Windows Server 2003 Checklist 5.1.6 Appendix A / A.3.

Review Guidelines
- When a new server is deployed, a server deployment checklist will be completed and submitted to InfoSec for approval. The checklist will be entered into the asset management system. (Appendix A)

- On a weekly basis, a baseline review will be preformed on all production servers in accordance with the Security Technical Implementation Guides (STIGS) WINDOWS 2003/XP/2000 ADDENDUM Version 5, Release 1, Section 2.1. Any irregularities will be promptly submitted to InfoSec.
- On a bi-annual basis, production server services will be audited, documented and reviewed by InfoSec. (Appendix B)

Appendix A
Server Deployment Checklist

This checklist will be completed and submitted to InfoSec when installing and configuring a new server.

After connecting to the network:

Action	Notes	Status
Place the server in the applicable production OU.		
Force Group Policy update by executing "gpupdate /force."		
Execute "gpresult" to validate that the server role GPO is applied.		
Once the GPO is applied, execute "gpresult > <Server Name>gpresult.txt" and attach the file to server's properties in the asset management system.		
Confirm that anti-virus software is enabled, configured, and updated.		
Run a MBSA scan from the host to audit for compliance.		
Run a Nmap scan against the host to audit for compliance.		

Appendix B
Server services audit.

Service	Purpose	Installed	Disabled
Alerter	Alerter: Creates pop-up messages from the system when services fail to start (etc.). Requires Messenger service.		
ClipBook Server	Clipbook Server: Serves up local clipbook pages to other Clipbook Viewers.		
Computer Browser	Computer Browser: Allows for viewing of other computers and resources on the network.		
DHCP Client	DHCP client: will automatically contact the DHCP server (Port 67) to acquire the needed network configuration.		
Directory Replicator	Directory Replicator: When configured, will replicate files and directories to other machines.		
Messenger	Messenger: Used to send messages to users or machines and sends messages from the Alerter service.		
Net Logon	Net Logon: Part of the security subsystem, enabling user authentication as well as keeping domain security in sync.		
Network DDE	Network DDE: Transport for Dynamic Data Exchange traffic, used by standard Office applications when sharing data over a network.		
Network DDE DSDM	Network DDE DSDM: DDE Share Database Manager, used by Network DDE service.		
Plug and Play	Plug and Play		

Remote Procedure Call (RPC) Locator	Remote Procedure Call Locator: Used by RPC applications to register availability of resources, and by clients to find compatible RPC server applications.		
Server	Server: Used to provide file and print resources to the network.		
SNMP Trap Service	SNMP Trap Service: Used by network administrators to monitor and to reach remote devices.		
Spooler (unless you need to spool printing)	Spooler: Stores print jobs and queues them to be printed.		
TCP/IP NetBIOS Helper	NetBIOS Helper: Passes normal TCP/IP connection requests to the sockets interface to allow NetBIOS resolution.		
Telephony Service	Telephony Service: Enables a telephony card or phone system to understand commands from an application via the operating system.		
Workstation (Required for Raptor Firewall)	Workstation: Manages connections to network resources such as drive mappings, printer connections, etc.		
Event Log	Event Log: Responsible for creating entries in the Event logs.		
NT LM Security Support Provider	NT LM Security Support: The LSA handles all authentications before a user is allowed to access a resource.		
Remote Procedure Call (RPC) Service	RPC (RPC) Service: Name service provider that maintains a database with available RPC services on the server, where local RPC services		

	can register themselves. A client can then contact the RPC locator on the server to locate and access the wanted RPC service.		
Schedule	Schedule: Used to run applications or batch/command files at specific times, using the "at" command.		
UPS	UPS: Generic uninterruptible power supply service, which shuts the machine down during a power failure.		

Appendix C.
Logon Message:

UNAUTHORIZED USE OF THIS SYSTEM IS PROHIBITED
NOTICE TO USERS

This computer is the private property of <Company Name>. It is for authorized use only.

<Company Name> reserves the right to monitor its use as necessary to ensure its stability, availability and security. During monitoring, information may be examined, recorded, copied and used for authorized purposes. Use of this computer system constitutes consent to this policy and the policies and procedures set forth by <Company Name>. Unauthorized or improper use of this system may result in civil and criminal penalties and administrative or disciplinary action, as appropriate.

****

Policy Review
This policy will be reviewed bi-annually.

Compliance
Any employee found to have violated this policy may be subject to disciplinary action, up to and including termination of employment.

Related Policies, Standards, and Guidelines
Security Technical Implementation Guides (STIGS) WINDOWS 2003/XP/2000 ADDENDUM Version 5, Release 1, Section 2.1.
Media Disposal Policy
Intrusion Response Plan
Change Management Policy
Log Configuration Standards
<Server Role Name> Baseline Configuration

Chapter 9 Summary
This chapter reviewed a tier 3 Windows Server Security Policy. The example policy shows how organizations use the policy to define their

Windows server security and minimum server standards. The policy defined General Guidelines, Windows Server Configuration Guidelines, Patch Update Guidelines, File System Guidelines, Review Guidelines and Appendixes that provide an authorized framework to provision Windows servers into a production environment.

- Windows Server Security Policy defines an organization's Windows server security and minimum server standards.
- Windows server and desktop operating systems have integrated operating system and networking functions that provide a wide variety of security configurations to secure both the operating system and networking functions.
- Many organizations develop, test and support a single, generic server build, which becomes a baseline for all of their servers.
- As new servers are provisioned, policies govern the configuration and management of the server role.

The next chapter will review a Terminal Server Configuration Baseline.

Reference
Security Technical Implementation Guides (STIG) "Windows 2003/XP/2000 Addendum V5R1"

Chapter 10: Terminal Server Installation Baseline

Chapter Overview:

This chapter reviews a tier 3 Terminal Server Installation Baseline. A Terminal Server Installation Baseline provides employees with an approved procedure to install Terminal Server. It is used with other IT infrastructure policies to address interoperability and security of Terminal Server in the context of the entire information system. For example, in Chapter 6, the IT Server Room Security Policy defined physical and environmental security; Chapter 7, the Password Policy defined password requirements; Chapter 8, the Windows Terminal Server Standards policy defined Terminal Server Standards, and in Chapter 9, the Windows Server Security Policy defined an operating system baseline security configuration for all new servers. Together these policies reduce risk by implementing layered security controls (defense in depth) through the Enterprise.

Installing the Terminal Server role allows users to connect to a Terminal Server by using an RDP client. The installation is a quick and simple process that enables Terminal Services. The installation can be made using the *Manage Your Server* applet or from *Add and Remove Programs*.

The installation with the *Manage Your Server* applet provides a streamlined installation process that automatically configures a Terminal server in Full Security permission mode. The *Add and Remove Programs* installation method offers an additional window in which it is possible to select between Full Security, which is selected by default or Relaxed Security. The permission mode can be changed after the installation with the Terminal Services Configuration applet.

The permission settings dictate the default permissions for users accessing system files and registry keys. With Full Security, non-administrators cannot modify the HKEY_LOCAL_MACHINE registry key or write files to the server's hard drive other than their profile directory. Full Security effectively restricts permissions for Terminal Server users to the "Users Group" permissions. The Relaxed Security setting provides Terminal Server users with quasi Power User access to system folders and registry keys. Relaxed Security is commonly used as a quick fix to enable legacy or poorly written applications to operate on Windows Server 2003.

A default Windows Server 2003 Terminal Server installation employs a default deny strategy by restricting system access exclusively to administrators. Users or groups must be explicitly added to each Terminal Server's local Remote Desktop Users group in order to be granted logon rights to a Terminal Server.

From a security perspective, it is important to consider the permission mode and the membership of the Remote Desktop Users group. Ideally, all Terminal Servers should be in Full Security mode in order to protect the server from unauthorized access. In the event that a particular application will not run in Full Security mode, first troubleshoot the application on a test server in Full Security mode to determine and resolve the root cause before considering using Relaxed Security. Membership in the Remote Desktop Users group provides explicit access control to a Terminal Server environment. A best practice to manage Remote Desktop Users group membership is to create and audit a security group that contains only approved Terminal Server user accounts. This group is then added to the Remote Desktop Users group on each server to grant access.

List 10.1 shows prerequisites and assumptions for installing Terminal Server:
- The server will comply with all appropriate IT infrastructure policies, such as IT Server Room Security Policy, Windows Terminal Server Standards, Windows Server Security Policy, and so forth.
- All Terminal Servers are grouped together in an Organizational Unit.
- All Terminal Servers are Windows Server 2003 Service Pack 2.

The following example is a tier 3 Terminal Server Installation Baseline that is used by employees to install Terminal Server. This example is intended for informational purposes only.

Terminal Server Installation Baseline

Purpose
The purpose of this baseline is to define standards for the installation of Terminal Services. Before any servers are placed on the production network, standard processes will be executed to ensure that all servers are installed and maintained in a manner that prevents unauthorized access, unauthorized use and disruptions in service

Scope
This baseline is specifically for any Windows Terminal Server on the internal network and will be reviewed in conjunction with the other IT infrastructure policies.

Terminal Server Installation Baseline
1. Log on to the target Terminal Server as administrator.
2. Click Start > Programs > Administrative Tools > Configure your Server Wizard, and then click the "Add or remove a role" link. Click **Next** from the Preliminary Steps window.
3. From the Server Role window, select the "Terminal server" role and click **Next**. **Note:** All other options should be set to **No**.
4. Follow the remaining portion of the Wizard and restart the machine when prompted.
5. After the server is restarted, log on as Administrator and click **Finish** and close the Help menu.

Policy Review
This policy will be reviewed annually.

Compliance
Any employee found to have violated this policy may be subject to disciplinary action, up to and including termination of employment.

Related Policies, Standards, and Guidelines
Change Management Policy
<Server Role Name> Baseline Security Configuration

Chapter 10 Summary
This chapter began with a discussion about a Terminal Server Installation Baseline, followed by an overview the Terminal Server installation process. The chapter concluded with an example Terminal Server Installation Baseline.

- A Terminal Server Installation Baseline provides employees with an approved procedure to install Terminal Server and is used together with other IT infrastructure policies to address interoperability and security of Terminal Server.
- Installing the Terminal Server role allows users to connect to a Terminal Server using an RDP client.
- The installation can be made using the *Manage Your Server* applet or from *Add and Remove Programs*.
- It is important to consider the permission settings (Full Security or Relaxed Security) and Remote Desktop Users group membership in a Terminal Server environment.
- The permission settings dictate the default permissions for users accessing system files and registry keys.
- With Full Security, non-administrators cannot modify the HKEY_LOCAL_MACHINE registry key or write files to the server's hard drive other than to their profile directory.
- The Relaxed Security setting provides Terminal Server users with quasi Power User access to system folders and registry keys.
- Auditing membership of the Remote Desktop Users group provides explicit access control to a Terminal Server environment.

Chapter 11: Terminal Server Security Baseline

Chapter Overview:
This chapter will introduce a Terminal Server Security Baseline that is intended for educational purposes in order to provide guidance to develop a security baseline to meet your organization's specific requirements. The chapter begins with a review of how a Terminal Server Security Baseline relates to other IT infrastructure policies and then gives a short overview of Server Role configurations, general Terminal Server security configurations, Terminal Server Desktop security, prerequisites, and assumptions. It concludes with an example Terminal Server Security Baseline.

The development of a production Terminal Server Security Baseline requires extensive testing to ensure that applications function properly and that the user environment is not too restrictive in that it hampers user productivity. Each organization should evaluate its unique requirements in order to develop a security baseline that provides sufficient security and manageability, without limiting user productivity.

Organizations develop baselines to introduce Quality Assurance (QA) and reduce risk associated with the installation and configuration of technologies. A Terminal Server Security Baseline is one of many layered policies within the Platform Architecture Domain that is used with other IT infrastructure policies to address interoperability and security of Terminal Server in the context of the entire Enterprise. The Terminal Server Security Baseline relies on other IT infrastructure policies to provide security controls at each step of provisioning a Terminal Server and at each layer of the IT infrastructure. Together these policies reduce risk by implementing layered security controls (defense in depth) throughout the Enterprise. A Terminal Server

Security Baseline is a process that can be reliably duplicated, audited or modified to meet evolving business and regulatory requirements.

Terminal Server Security Baselines tend to be large documents that cover server role configurations, Terminal Server security configurations and Terminal Server Desktop security. The next three sections will highlight each portion of the example Terminal Server Security Baselines. First, we will review the Server Role configurations and Terminal Server security configurations. These will be followed by the Terminal Server Desktop security section.

Server Role Configurations with the Microsoft Security Configuration Wizard

This section of the example baselines runs through the procedure to create a Terminal Server security role using the Microsoft Security Configuration Wizard. There are many third party solutions to develop security policies, but we selected the Microsoft Security Configuration Wizard because of its availability, acceptance and cost. The Security Configuration Wizard is bundled with Windows Server 2003 with Service Pack 1 and is well documented and widely adopted.

Microsoft calls the Security Configuration Wizard "an attack-surface reduction tool for Windows Server 2003 with Service Pack 1 family of products." The Security Configuration Wizard supports a GUI and command line interface for the development of server security policies. It leverages Windows 2003 roles-based infrastructure to determine which ports and services need to be enabled for a given server role.

While developing a security policy, the server role's minimum requirements are defined by disabling functionality that is not required. The security policy disables unneeded services, blocks unused ports, reduces protocol exposure and defines a high signal-to-noise audit ratio. The Security Configuration Wizard generates security policies as an XML file and the command-line utility can be used to convert an XML file into a Group Policy Object. Once the Group Policy Object is created, it must be linked to the target Organizational Unit. Security policies can be applied locally in XML format or centrally via Group Policy Objects.

Developing a security policy is broken down into four sections. These sections are organized and referenced in the Security Configuration Wizard user interface, using a security configuration database structure. Once the security configuration database is processed, it can be viewed or printed using the Security Configuration Wizard Viewer. The Wizard walks through the Server Role, Network Security, Registry Settings, Audit Policy and Internet Information Services (if installed) sections related to the server's roles and functions.

The Security Configuration Wizard walks through the following sections and sub-sections:

Server Roles
- Client Features
- Administration and Other Options
- Additional Services
- Handling Unspecified Services

Network Security
- Open Ports and Approved Applications

Registry Settings
- Require SMB Security Signatures
- Outbound Authentication Methods
- Inbound Authentication Methods

Audit Policy
- Do Not Audit
- Audit Successful Activities
- Audit Successful and Unsuccessful Activities

Internet Information Services
- Web Service Extensions for Dynamic Content
- Virtual Directories to Retain
- Prevent Anonymous Users from Accessing Content Files

Server Roles Configuration
This section allows the configuration of installed and available services based on the server's role. The Wizard does not install

components or set up a server like the *Configure Your Server Wizard* does. Instead, it will enable services and open ports based on a list of server roles and client features.

Network security
This section is designed to configure inbound ports using the Windows Firewall. The configuration is based on the roles and administration options selected in the Server Role section. It is possible to restrict access to ports and configure port traffic to be signed or encrypted using IPSec. This section will be skipped in the example because the Windows Firewall is not installed.

Registry settings
This section addresses the configuration of the protocols used to communicate with other computers on the network. This section allows a server to be configured in order to reduce protocol exposure when communicating with legacy Windows operating systems. Communication with legacy Windows operating systems uses protocols that are vulnerable to password cracking and man-in-the-middle attacks.

Audit policy
This section allows the configuration of system auditing based on organizational auditing requirements. The audit policy can be configured not to audit any events, to audit only successful events, or to audit both successful and unsuccessful events. The audit policy not only configures the Object Access events but also the entire audit policy list of events.

Internet Information Services (IIS)
This section is displayed only if IIS is installed. This section allows the configuration of the security aspects of Internet Information Services (IIS). This section will be skipped in the example because IIS is not installed.

Terminal Server Security Configurations
This section of the Terminal Server Security Baselines will review the procedure to implement the security controls from Appendix B of the Windows 2003/XP/2000 Addendum Version 5, Release 1 STIG and

the recommended restrictive settings from Microsoft "Locking Down Windows Server 2003 Terminal Server Sessions" white paper. All of the STIGs configurations and the Microsoft recommendations will be implemented using Group Policy.

The Security Technical Implementation Guides (STIGS) and the NSA Guides are the configuration standards for the U. S. Department of Defense (DoD) Information Assurance (IA) and Information Assurance-enabled devices and systems. Appendix B of the Windows 2003/XP/2000 Addendum Version 5, Release 1 STIG addressed the Department of Defense's minimum security requirements for Terminal Server. Appendix B is broken into nine sections.

List 11.1 shows the sections in Appendix B.
- B.1 Terminal Services
- B.2 Windows Installer
- B.3 Windows Messenger
- B.4 Logon
- B.5 Group Policy
- B.6 Windows Time Service
- B.7 Network Connections
- B.8 Installation of Printers Using Kernel-mode Drivers
- B.9 Media Player – Automatic Downloads

Note: B.6 will not be included in the example Baseline.

In addition to the STIG, an extensive list of recommended restrictive settings can be found in a Microsoft white paper named "Locking Down Windows Server 2003 Terminal Server Sessions." Not all of the setting from the STIG and Microsoft's white paper are necessary; therefore organizations should evaluate and test all of the settings to determine if they are too restrictive for their environment. Enabling all of the settings will create a restrictive environment that may make the environment challenging to manage and hinder user productivity.

In addition to the setting in Appendix B of the Windows 2003/XP/2000 Addendum Version 5, Release 1 STIG and the recommended restrictive settings from Microsoft "Locking Down

Windows Server 2003 Terminal Server Sessions" white paper, there are additional Group Policy configurations that should be considered. For example, virtual channel restrictions and encryption levels should be evaluated to determine which settings meet an organization's specific requirements.

Table 11.1 lists security related virtual channel Group Policy settings. The settings can be configured with the Terminal Services Configuration utility (tscc.msc) or centrally via Active Directory from: Computer Configurations > Administrative Templates > Windows Components > Terminal Services > Client/Server data redirection

Table 11.1

Client/Server data redirection Setting	Explanation
Do not allow clipboard redirection	Determines if sharing of clipboard (cut and paste) contents between Terminal Server applications and local applications during a Terminal Server session should be disabled.
Allow audio redirection	By default Terminal Server on Windows Server 2003 disables audio redirection.
Do not allow COM port redirection	Determines if the mapping of client COM ports during a Terminal Server session should be disabled.
Do not allow client printer redirection	Determines if mapping of client printers during a Terminal Server session should be disabled.
Do not allow LPT port redirection	Determines if the redirection of data to client LPT ports during a Terminal Server session should be disabled.
Do not allow driver redirection	Determines if the mapping of client hard drives during a Terminal Server session should be disabled.

All of the RDP client encryption levels can be configured locally on a Terminal Server using the Terminal Services Configuration utility (tscc.msc) or centrally via Active Directory. Using Active Directory administrators can select between three setting: Client Compatible, High or Low. The Group Policies can be configured in Active Directory by editing the desired Group Policy Object in the following location:
Computer Configurations > Administrative Templates > Windows Components > Terminal Services > Encryption and Security.

Table 11.2 shows the client encryption settings.

Table 11.2

Setting	Explanation
FIPS	All data sent from client to server and the data sent from server to client is encrypted using the Federal Information Processing Standard (FIPS) encryption algorithms with Microsoft cryptographic modules. **Note:** FIPS encryption must be configured locally on each Terminal Server using the Terminal Services Configuration utility (tscc.msc).
Client compatible	All data that traverses between the client and the server is encrypted based on the maximum key strength supported by the client.
High	All data that traverses between the client and the server is encrypted based on the server's maximum key strength. Clients who do not support this level of encryption cannot connect.
Low	All data that traverses between the client and the server is protected by encryption based on the maximum key strength supported by the client.
Disabled or Not Configured	If the setting is Disabled or Not Configured, the encryption level is not enforced via Group Policy. Note: Administrators can configure the encryption level on the server with the Terminal Services Configuration tool.

Terminal Server Desktop Security

This section of the Terminal Server Security Baselines will review the procedure to implement desktop security controls using Group Policy. The main objective of desktop security is to provide standardization, security and compliance. Desktop security controls for Terminal Server ensure that the Terminal Server desktop environment is secured in a way to protect the operating system and network from unauthorized user access. For example, access to the Control Panel, Start Menu, Taskbar and Desktop options should be individually evaluated and configured to protect the operating system and network from user access.

There are various user level Group Policy Object settings that provide control over Control Panel, Start Menu, Taskbar and Desktop options. Figure 11.1 show the location of the Group Policy Objects to configure Control Panel, Start Menu, Taskbar and Desktop options.

Figure 11.1

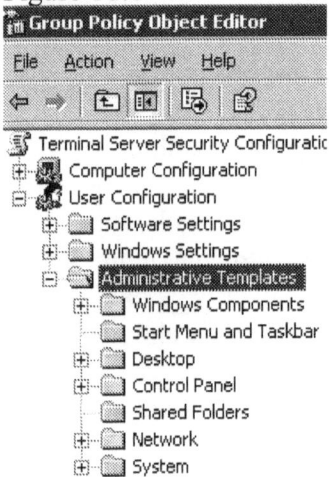

Implementing desktop security controls requires substantial testing in a lab or pilot environment to ensure that the desktop is adequately secured while not effecting user productivity.

Prerequisites and Assumptions

List 11.2 shows the prerequisites and assumptions to develop and apply the Terminal Server Security Baseline.

List 11.2

Part 1. Server Role Configurations

- For security reasons, the example server role disables Remote Windows Administration. To enable remote administration in the Security Configuration Wizard, select the "Remote Windows Administration" from the Select Administration and Other Options window.
- When testing a baseline, the target test or pilot Terminal Server will be provisioned identical as the production Terminal Servers.
- Validate and inventory all required anti-virus services.
- Validate and inventory all required anti-virus inbound ports.
- All applications will be tested and validated against the security profile before a production GPO is validated, named and deployed to production.

Part 2. Terminal Server Security Configurations

- Client/Server data redirection and encryption level configurations will be reviewed to determine which settings will be implemented.
- Server scalability metrics will be validated to determine the maximum sessions per server. The metric is necessary to implement Appendix B, Section B.1.3 of the Windows 2003/XP/2000 Addendum Version 5, Release 1 STIG.
  - o By default, Terminal Servers allow an unlimited number of connections that allow a potential for denial of service (DoS) attacks.
- Windows Messenger usage will be reviewed to determine which security controls outlined in Appendix B, Section B.3.0 of the Windows 2003/XP/2000 Addendum Version 5, Release 1 STIG will be implemented.
- The Windows Time Service will be reviewed to determine how to implement Appendix B, Section B.6 of the Windows 2003/XP/2000 Addendum Version 5, Release 1 STIG.
  - o The Windows Time service maintains date and time synchronization for Windows 2000XP/2003 machines. Time synchronization is used to ensure the security of Kerberos authentication within an Active Directory

environment. Synching to a reliable time source can reduce the risk of replay attacks.

- Folder redirection will be implemented for Application Data, Desktop, My Documents and the Start Menu.
- All GPO settings will be validated in a lab environment before deployed into production.

Part 3. Desktop Security

- When testing the desktop security controls, the target test or pilot Terminal Server will be provisioned identical as the production Terminal Servers.

Tip: While developing policies, it is possible to lock yourself and users out of the machine. A quick way to circumvent policies is to reboot the machine into safe mode. While in safe mode, policies are not applied and administrative capabilities will be restored. Edit the policy, execute "gpupdate", and then restart the computer.

The following example is a tier 3 Terminal Server Security Baseline that will create a secure restrictive environment. The example baseline starts with a Purpose and Scope statement, which is followed by the procedure to create an XML template for a Windows Server 2003 Terminal Server with the Security Configuration Wizard, export it as a GPO and then link it to the Terminal Server Organizational Unit. Next is the configuration of the security controls from Appendix B of the Windows 2003/XP/2000 Addendum Version 5, Release 1 STIG, followed by the recommended restrictive computer and users settings from Microsoft's "Locking Down Windows Server 2003 Terminal Server Sessions" white paper. The final section reviews the configuration of desktop security controls. The baseline concludes with the Policy Review, Compliance and Related Policies, Standards, and Guidelines statements. This baseline is intended for informational purposes only.

Terminal Server Security Baseline

Purpose
The purpose of this baseline is to define a security baseline for all Terminal Servers. Before any servers are placed on the production network, standard processes will be executed to ensure that all servers

are installed and maintained in a manner that prevents unauthorized access, unauthorized use and disruptions in service.

Scope
This baseline is for all Windows Terminal Servers on the internal network and will be reviewed in conjunction with the other IT infrastructure policies. This baseline is divided into two sections: Server Role Configurations and Terminal Server Security Configurations.

Terminal Server Security Baseline
1.0 Server Role Configurations
The following procedure will create a XML template for a Windows Server 2003 Terminal Server, using the Security Configuration Wizard. Export it as a GPO and then link it to the Terminal Server Organizational Unit.

The template will be created, tested and validated in a lab or pilot environment on a test server. The test server will be provisioned identically as production Terminal Servers. All of the template settings will be validated against each production application with test users. While testing templates, the revision number will be appended to the end of the file name, such as WTS_DEV01, WTS_DEV02, and so forth. Once a template is validated, it will be named WTS_Prod_month/day/year and placed in production. Template modifications will be made using the Security Configuration Wizard option of "Edit an existing security policy."

1. Log on to the target Terminal Server as administrator.
2. Click Start > Run, type "scw.exe" in the text area, and then click **OK** to access the Security Configuration Wizard.
3. From the Welcome window, click **Next** to proceed.
4. From the Configuration Action window, select the "Create a new security policy" radio button. Click **Next** to proceed.
5. From the Select Server window, enter the "FQDN" of the local host. Click **Next** to proceed.
6. From the Processing Security Configuration Database window, wait until the database has processed. Click **Next** to proceed.

7. From the Role-Based Service Configuration window, click **Next** to proceed.
8. From the Select Server Roles window, select only "Terminal Server." Click **Next** to proceed.
9. From the Select Client Features window, select the following:
   - Automatic update client
   - DNS client
   - DNS registration client
   - Domain member
   - Microsoft networking client
   - WINS client

Click **Next** to proceed.

10. From the Select Administrator and Other Options window, select the following:
    - Application Experience Lookup Service
    - Application installation from Group Policy
    - Terminal Server Printer Redirection

Click **Next** to proceed.

11. From the Select Additional Services window, select the desired anti-virus services. Click **Next** to proceed.
12. From the Handle Unspecified Services window, set the policy to "Do not change startup mode of the service." Click **Next** to proceed.
13. From the Confirm Services Changes window, click **Next** to proceed.
14. From the Network Security window, select the "Skip this section" check box. Click **Next** to proceed.
15. From the Registry Settings window, ensure that the "Skip this section" is unchecked. Click **Next** to proceed.
16. From the Required SMB Security Signatures window, unselect both options. Click **Next** to proceed.
17. From the Outbound Authentication Methods window, unselect all of the options. Click **Next** to proceed.
18. From the Inbound Authentication Methods window, unselect all of the options. Click **Next** to proceed.
19. From the Registry Settings Summary window, click **Next** to proceed.
20. From the Audit Policy window, ensure that the "Skip this section" is unchecked. Click **Next** to proceed.

21. From the System Audit Policy window, select "Audit successful and unsuccessful activities." Click **Next** to proceed.
22. From the Audit Policy Summary window, select the "Also include the Security Configuration Wizard Audit.inf security template" check box. Click **Next** to proceed.
23. From the Save Security Policy window, click **Next** to proceed.
24. From the Security Policy File Name window, accept the default path and type the template file name (i.e. C:\WINDOWS\Security\msscw\Policies\WTS_Prod_ month/day/year). Click **Next** to proceed.
25. From the Apply Security Policy window, select the "Apply now" radio button. Click **Next** to proceed.
26. From the Completing the Security Configuration Wizard window, click **Finish** to conclude the procedure.

Terminal Server Security Baseline
1.1 Server Role Configurations, Convert security policy file into a GPO.

1   Log on to a domain member server as an administrator that has the Group Policy Management Console and the Security Configuration Wizard.
2   From a command prompt type: "scwcmd transform /p:PathToPolicyFile /g:DesiredGPODisplayName"
   • PathToPolicyFile is the production policy file created with the Security Configuration Wizard, including its .xml file extension.
   • DesiredGPODisplayName is the name of the Group Policy Object as it appears in Group Policy Object Editor or in Group Policy Management Console.
3   Open the Group Policy Management console. In the left pane, expand the "forest and domain" nodes and select the "WTS Organizational Unit." Right click the "WTS Organizational Unit" and link the GPO created in step 2 (the above step) to complete the procedure.

Terminal Server Security Baseline

Part 2. Terminal Server Security Configurations (Source: Appendix B of the Windows 2003/XP/2000 Addendum Version 5, Release 1 STIG)

1   Log on to a domain member server with the Group Policy Management Console as an administrator.

2   Open the Group Policy Management Console. In the left pane, expand the forest and domain nodes. Then expand the WTS Organizational Unit and right click the "WTS_Prod_ month/day/year" GPO and click **edit**. Add the following settings:

3   Computer Configurations > Administrative Templates > System > Group Policy and **enable** the "Use Group Policy loopback processing mode" policy.

4   B.1.1. Computer Configurations > Administrative Templates > Windows Components > Terminal Services and **disable** the "Keep-Alive Connections" policy.

5   B.1.2. Computer Configurations > Administrative Templates > Windows Components > Terminal Services and **enable** the "Restrict Terminal server users to a single remote session" policy.

6   B.1.3. Computer Configurations > Administrative Templates > Windows Components > Terminal Services and **enable** the "Limit number of connections" policy to "<number of maximum connections allowed>."

7   B.1.4. Computer Configurations > Administrative Templates > Windows Components > Terminal Services > Temporary folders and **disable** the "Do not use temp folders per Session" policy.

8   B.1.5. Computer Configurations > Administrative Templates > Windows Components > Terminal Services > Temporary folders and **disable** the "Do not delete temp folder upon exit" policy.

9   B.1.6. Computer Configurations > Administrative Templates > Windows Components > Terminal Services > Sessions and **enable** the "Set a time limit for active but idle Terminal Services sessions" policy and set the idle session limit to "15 minutes."

10 B.1.7. Computer Configurations > Administrative Templates > Windows Components > Terminal Services > Sessions and **enable** the "Terminate session when time limits are reached" policy.

11 B.2.1. Computer Configurations > Administrative Templates > Windows Components > Windows Installer and **disable** the "Always install with elevated privileges" policy.

12 B.2.1. User Configurations > Administrative Templates > Windows Components > Windows Installer and **disable** the "Always install with elevated privileges" policy.

13 B.2.2. Computer Configurations > Administrative Templates > Windows Components > Windows Installer and **disable** the "Disable IE security prompt for Windows Installer scripts" policy.

14 B.2.3. Computer Configurations > Administrative Templates > Windows Components > Windows Installer and **disable** the "Enable user control over installs" policy.

15 B.2.4. Computer Configurations > Administrative Templates > Windows Components > Windows Installer and **disable** the "Enable user to browse for source while elevated" policy.

16 B.2.5. Computer Configurations > Administrative Templates > Windows Components > Windows Installer and **disable** the "Enable user to use media source while elevated" policy.

17 B.2.6. Computer Configurations > Administrative Templates > Windows Components > Windows Installer and **disable** the "Enable user to patch elevated products" policy.

18 B.2.7. Computer Configurations > Administrative Templates > Windows Components > Windows Installer and **disable** the "Allow admin to install from Terminal Services session" policy.

19 B.2.8. Computer Configurations > Administrative Templates > Windows Components > Windows Installer and **enable** the "Cache transforms in secure location on workstation" policy.

20 B.3. Computer Configurations > Administrative Templates > Windows Components > Windows Messenger and **enable** the "Do not allow Windows Messenger to be run" policy.

21 B.3.1. Computer Configurations > Administrative Templates > Windows Components >Windows Messenger and **enable** the "Do not automatically start Windows Messenger initially" policy.

22 B.5. Computer Configurations > Administrative Templates > System > Group Policy and **disable** the "Turn off background refresh of Group Policy" policy.

23 B.7.1. Computer Configurations > Administrative Templates > Network > Network Connections and **enable** the "Prohibit use of Internet Connection Sharing on your DNS domain network" policy.

24 B.7.2. Computer Configurations > Administrative Templates > Network > Network Connections and **enable** the "Prohibit

installation and configuration of Network Bridge on your DNS domain network" policy.

25 B.9. Computer Configurations > Administrative Templates > Windows Components > Windows Media Player and **enable** the "Prevent Automatic Updates" policy.

26 B.9. User Configurations > Administrative Templates > Windows Components > Windows Media Player > Playback and **enable** the "Prevent Codec Download" policy.

Terminal Server Security Baseline
Part 2.1 Terminal Server Security Configurations (Source: Microsoft's white paper "Locking Down Windows Server 2003 Terminal Server Sessions")

1. Computer Configuration > Windows Settings > Security Settings > Local Policies > Security Options and **enable** the "Devices: Restrict CD-ROM access to locally logged-on user only" policy.

2. Computer Configuration > Windows Settings > Security Settings > Local Policies > Security Options and **enable** the "Devices: Restrict floppy access to locally logged-on user only" policy.

3. Computer Configuration > Windows Settings > Security Settings > Local Policies > Security Options and **enable** the "Interactive logon: Do not display last user name" policy.

4. Computer Configuration > Windows Settings > Security Settings > System Services and **disable** the "Help and Support" policy.

5. Computer Configuration > Administrative Templates > Windows Components > Terminal Services > Client/Server data redirection and **enable** the "Do not allow drive redirection" policy.

6. User Configuration > Windows Settings > Folder Redirection and right click the "Application Data" node to access its properties. Recommended setting: "Basic redirection" and "Create a folder for each user under the root path." Enter the desired Root Path. On the **Settings** tab, **enable** "Grant the user exclusive rights to Application Data." **Enable** "Move contents of Application Data folder to new location." Set the policy removal to "Redirect the folder back to the local user profile location when policy is removed."

7. User Configuration > Windows Settings > Folder Redirection and right click the "Desktop" node to access its properties.

Recommended setting: "Basic redirection" and "Create a folder for each user under the root path." Enter the desired Root Path. On the **Settings** tab, **enable** "Grant the user exclusive rights to Desktop." **Enable** "Move contents of Desktop to the new location." Set the policy removal to "Redirect the folder back to the local user profile location when policy is removed."

8. User Configuration > Windows Settings > Folder Redirection and right click the "My Documents" node to access its properties. Recommended setting: "Basic redirection" and "Create a folder for each user under the root path." Enter the desired Root Path. On the **Settings** tab, **enable** "Grant the user exclusive rights to My Documents." **Enable** "Move contents of My Documents to the new location." Set the policy removal to "Redirect the folder back to the local user profile location when policy is removed."

9. User Configuration > Windows Settings > Folder Redirection and right click the "Start Menu" node to access its properties. Recommended setting: "Basic redirection" and "Redirect to the following location." Enter the desired Root Path. On the **Settings** tab, set the policy removal to "Redirect the folder back to the local user profile location when the policy is removed."

10. User Configuration > Administrative Templates > Windows Components > Internet Explorer and **enable** the "Search: Disable Find Files via F3 within the browser" policy.

11. User Configuration > Administrative Templates > Windows Components > Internet Explorer > Browser menus and **enable** the "Disable Context menu" policy.

12. User Configuration > Administrative Templates > Windows Components > Application Compatibility and **enable** the "Prevent access to 16-bit applications" policy.

13. User Configuration > Administrative Templates > Windows Components > Windows Explorer and **enable** the "Removes the Folder Options menu item from the Tools menu" policy.

14. User Configuration > Administrative Templates > Windows Components > Windows Explorer and **enable** the "Remove File menu from Windows Explorer" policy.

15. User Configuration > Administrative Templates > Windows Components > Windows Explorer and **enable** the "Remove Map Network Drive and Disconnect Network Drive" policy.

16. User Configuration > Administrative Templates > Windows Components > Windows Explorer and **enable** the "Remove Search button from Windows Explorer" policy.

17. User Configuration > Administrative Templates > Windows Components > Windows Explorer and **enable** the "Remove Security Tab" policy.

18. User Configuration > Administrative Templates > Windows Components > Windows Explorer and **enable** the "Remove Windows Explorer's default context menu" policy.

19. User Configuration > Administrative Templates > Windows Components > Windows Explorer and **enable** the "Hides the Manage item on the Windows Explorer shortcut menu" policy.

20. User Configuration > Administrative Templates > Windows Components > Windows Explorer and **enable** the "Hide these specified drives in My Computer" policy and then select "Enabled – Restrict all drives."

21. User Configuration > Administrative Templates > Windows Components > Windows Explorer and **enable** the "Prevent access to drives from My Computer" policy and then select "Enabled – Restrict all drives."

22. User Configuration > Administrative Templates > Windows Components > Windows Explorer and **enable** the "Remove Hardware tab" policy.

23. User Configuration > Administrative Templates > Windows Components > Windows Explorer and **enable** the "Remove Order Prints from Picture Tasks" policy.

24. User Configuration > Administrative Templates > Windows Components > Windows Explorer and **enable** the "Remove Publish to Web from File and Folders Tasks" policy.

25. User Configuration > Administrative Templates > Windows Components > Windows Explorer and **enable** the "No "Computers Near Me" in My Network Places" policy.

26. User Configuration > Administrative Templates > Windows Components > Windows Explorer and **enable** the "No "Entire Network" in My Network Places" policy.

27. User Configuration > Administrative Templates > Windows Components > Windows Explorer and **enable** the "Turn off Windows+X hotkeys" policy.

28. User Configuration > Administrative Templates > Windows Components > Windows Explorer and **enable** the "Turn on Classic Shell" policy.
29. User Configuration > Administrative Templates > Windows Components > Windows Explorer > Common Open File Dialog and **enable** the "Hide the common dialog places bar" policy.
30. User Configuration > Administrative Templates > Windows Components > Task Scheduler and **enable** the "Hide Property Pages" policy.
31. User Configuration > Administrative Templates > Windows Components > Task Scheduler and **enable** the "Prohibit New Task Creation" policy.
32. User Configuration > Administrative Templates > Windows Components > Windows Update and **enable** the "Remove access to use all Windows Update features" policy.
33. User Configuration > Administrative Templates > Start Menu & Taskbar and **enable** the "Remove links and access to Windows Update" policy.
34. User Configuration > Administrative Templates > Start Menu & Taskbar and **enable** the "Remove common program groups from Start Menu" policy.
35. User Configuration > Administrative Templates > Start Menu & Taskbar and **enable** the "Remove pinned programs list from Start Menu" policy.
36. User Configuration > Administrative Templates > Start Menu & Taskbar and **enable** the "Remove programs on Settings menu" policy.
37. User Configuration > Administrative Templates > Start Menu & Taskbar and **enable** the "Remove Network Connections from Start Menu" policy.
38. User Configuration > Administrative Templates > Start Menu & Taskbar and **enable** the "Remove the Search menu from Start Menu" policy.
39. User Configuration > Administrative Templates > Start Menu & Taskbar and **enable** the "Remove Drag-and-Drop shortcut menus on Start Menu" policy.
40. User Configuration > Administrative Templates > Start Menu & Taskbar and **enable** the "Remove Favorites menu from Start Menu" policy.

41. User Configuration > Administrative Templates > Start Menu & Taskbar and **enable** the "Remove Help menu from Start Menu" policy.
42. User Configuration > Administrative Templates > Start Menu & Taskbar and **enable** the "Remove Run menu from Start Menu" policy.
43. User Configuration > Administrative Templates > Start Menu & Taskbar and **enable** the "Remove My Network Place icon from Start Menu" policy.
44. User Configuration > Administrative Templates > Start Menu & Taskbar and **enable** the "Add Logoff to Start Menu" policy.
45. User Configuration > Administrative Templates > Start Menu & Taskbar and **enable** the "Remove and prevent access to Shut Down command" policy.
46. User Configuration > Administrative Templates > Start Menu & Taskbar and **enable** the "Prevent changes to Taskbar and Start Menu settings" policy.
47. User Configuration > Administrative Templates > Start Menu & Taskbar and **enable** the "Remove access to the shortcut menus for the taskbar" policy.
48. User Configuration > Administrative Templates > Desktop and **enable** the "Remove Properties from My Documents shortcut menu" policy.
49. User Configuration > Administrative Templates > Desktop and **enable** the "Remove Properties from My Computer shortcut menu" policy.
50. User Configuration > Administrative Templates > Desktop and **enable** the "Remove Properties from Recycle Bin shortcut menu" policy.
51. User Configuration > Administrative Templates > Desktop and **enable** the "Hide My Network Places icon on desktop" policy.
52. User Configuration > Administrative Templates > Desktop and **enable** the "Prohibit user from changing My Documents path" policy.
53. User Configuration > Administrative Templates > Desktop and **enable** the "Remove My Computer icon on the desktop" policy.
54. User Configuration > Administrative Templates > Control Panel and **enable** the "Prohibit access to the Control Panel" policy.

55. User Configuration > Administrative Templates > Control Panel > Add or Remove Programs and **enable** the "Remove Add or Remove Programs" policy.
56. User Configuration > Administrative Templates > Control Panel > Printers and **enable** the "Prevent addition of printers" policy
57. User Configuration > Administrative Templates > System and **enable** the "Prevent access to the command prompt" policy and Set "Disable the command prompt script processing also" to **No**.
58. User Configuration > Administrative Templates > System and **enable** the "Prevent access to registry editing tools" policy.
59. User Configuration > Administrative Templates > System > CTRL+ALT+DEL Options and **enable** the "Remove Task Manager" policy.
60. User Configuration > Administrative Templates > System > Scripts and **enable** the "Run legacy logon scripts hidden" policy.

Terminal Server Security Baseline
Part 2.2 Desktop Security Controls

1. User Configuration > Administrative Templates > Control Panel > Prohibit access to the control panel and **enable** the policy.
2. User Configuration > Administrative Templates > Desktop > Active Desktop > Disable Active Desktop and **enable** the policy.
3. User Configuration > Administrative Templates > Start Menu and Taskbar > Remove common start menu groups from Start Menu and **enable** the policy.
4. User Configuration > Administrative Templates > Start Menu and Taskbar > Remove Network Connections from Start Menu and **enable** the policy.
5. User Configuration > Administrative Templates > Start Menu and Taskbar > Remove My Network Places icon from Start Menu and **enable** the policy.
6. User Configuration > Administrative Templates > Start Menu and Taskbar > Remove and prevent access to the Shut Down command and **enable** the policy.
7. User Configuration > Administrative Templates > Start Menu and Taskbar > Remove Set Program Access and Defaults from Start Menu and **enable** the policy.

8. Close the Group Policy properties and exit the Group Policy Management Console.

Policy Review
This policy will be reviewed bi-annually.

Compliance
Any employee found to have violated this policy may be subject to disciplinary action, up to and including termination of employment.

Related Policies, Standards, and Guidelines
Change Management Policy

Chapter 11 Summary
This chapter discussed a Terminal Server Security Baseline policy, its contents, and how it relates to other IT infrastructure policies. It highlighted Server Role Configurations using Microsoft's Security Configuration Wizard followed with an overview of Terminal Server Security Configurations from Appendix B of the Windows 2003/XP/2000 Addendum Version 5, Release 1 STIG and the recommended restrictive computer and users settings from Microsoft's "Locking Down Windows Server 2003 Terminal Server Sessions" white paper and Terminal Server desktop security controls. The chapter concluded with a review of an example Terminal Server Security Baseline.

Terminal Server Security Baseline
- The development of a Terminal Server Security Baseline requires extensive testing to ensure application operability and to validate that user restrictions do not hinder productivity.
- Organizations evaluate their unique requirements to develop a security baseline that provides sufficient security and manageability, without limiting productivity.
- Organizations develop baseline configurations to introduce Quality Assurance (QA) and reduce risk associated with the installation and configuration of technologies.

- Terminal Server Security Baselines typically cover Server Role configurations, Terminal Server Security configurations and Terminal Server desktop security controls.

Security Configuration Wizard

- Microsoft calls the Security Configuration Wizard "an attack-surface reduction tool for the Windows Server 2003 with Service Pack 1 family of products."
- The Security Configuration Wizard leverages Windows 2003's roles-based infrastructure to determine which ports and services need to be enabled for a given server role.
- While developing a security policy, the server role's minimum requirements are defined by disabling functionality that is not required.
- Developing a security policy is broken down into five sections: Server Role, Network Security, Registry Settings, Audit Policy, and Internet Information Services (if installed) sections related to the servers roles and functions.

Appendix B of the Windows 2003/XP/2000 Addendum Version 5, Release 1 STIG

- The Security Technical Implementation Guides (STIGS) and the NSA Guides are the configuration standards for the U. S. Department of Defense (DoD) Information Assurance (IA) and Information Assurance-enabled devices and systems.
- Appendix B of the Windows 2003/XP/2000 Addendum Version 5, Release 1 STIG addressed the Department of Defense's minimum security requirements for Terminal Server.
- Appendix B is broken into nine sections.
- Not all of the settings from the STIGS are necessary; therefore organizations should evaluate and test all of the settings to determine if they are too restrictive for their environment.

Locking Down Windows Server 2003 Terminal Server Sessions

- An extensive list of recommended restrictive settings can be found in a Microsoft white paper named "Locking Down Windows Server 2003 Terminal Server Sessions."

- Not all of the settings from Microsoft's white paper are necessary; therefore organizations should evaluate and test all of the settings to determine if they are too restrictive for their environment.

Terminal Server Desktop Security
- The main objectives of desktop security are to provide standardization, security and compliance.
- Desktop security controls for Terminal Server ensure that the Terminal Server desktop environment is secured in a way to protect the operating system and network from unauthorized user access.
- There are various user level Group Policy Object settings that provide control over Control Panel, Start Menu, Taskbar and Desktop options.

The next chapter will review two tier 3 Configuration Baselines, a Session Directory Configuration Baseline, and a Terminal Server Session Directory Group Policy Configuration Baseline.

Reference
Security Configuration Wizard Documentation:
http://www.microsoft.com/downloads/details.aspx?familyid=903fd496 -9eb9-4a45-aa00-3f2f20fd6171&displaylang=en
Microsoft white paper named "Locking Down Windows Server 2003 Terminal Server Sessions":
http://www.microsoft.com/windowsserver2003/techinfo/overview/lock down.mspx

Chapter 12: Software Restriction Policy Baseline

Chapter Overview:
This chapter starts with an overview of why organizations implement application access restrictions and then introduces Microsoft Software Restriction Policies. The chapter concludes with an example tier 3 Software Restriction Policy Baseline. This chapter explains why organizations employ application access restrictions and offers directions to plan and implement Software Restriction Policies in your Terminal Server environment.

Administrators quickly learn that providing users with full access to their computer results in policy violations, system stability and security issues. Offering users full access to their computer typically results in an increased number of help desk calls, licensing violations, and data loss. By implementing security controls that limit user access rights to computers shores up an organizations security posture by limiting accidental or deliberate damage to computers, applications and data.

List 12.1 shows which issues can be prevented by implementing security controls that limit user access rights to a computer:
- Prevent the installation of unauthorized software or devices.
- Prevent unauthorized use of company software.
- Prevent unlicensed software use.
- Prevent users from playing computer games while working.
- Prevent users from downloading and sharing unauthorized content.
- Prevent viruses and malware infection.
- Prevent data loss.
- Prevent users from conducting personal business on company time.
- Prevent network access abuse.
- Prevent system configuration problems.

Organizations turn to desktop security controls and application access restrictions to manage user access rights on computers, enforce corporate policy, reduce system configuration problems and decrease system downtime. As discussed in Chapter 11, Terminal Server desktop security controls ensure that the desktop environment is properly secured in order to encourage accepted system usage. Application access restrictions promote standardized application usage by allowing administrators to define what applications and file types can or cannot be executed on a computer.

As discussed in Chapter 2, the default behavior with Terminal Server is to assume that all users have access to all applications installed on a Terminal Server. To meet business and regulatory requirements, many organizations turn to application access restrictions to define which applications are available to specific users. There are two strategies used to implement application restrictions: a black-list policy and a white-list policy. A black-list policy is one in which an administrator specifies which applications are not allowed to execute, and all other applications are allowed. A white-list policy is one which an administrator specifies which applications are allowed to execute, and all other applications are denied.

Software Restriction Policies

Microsoft Software Restriction Policies provide the integrated framework to implement granular application and file execution entitlements, using Active Directory Group Policy without the need of any additional 3rd party software. It was first introduced with Windows XP and followed by Windows Server 2003. Software Restriction Policies provide the security controls to manage application and file execution entitlements as well as the ability to mitigate the introduction of hostile code through email or web browsing, such as script based viruses or Active X controls. Script based viruses are controlled by the integration of the Windows scripting host with Software Restriction Policies, which provide control over VB Script and Jscript execution.

Software Restriction Policies are created using the Group Policy Management Console and can be applied to local machines, sites and domains, or Organizational Units. Software Restriction Policies can be configured as a user or machine policy. Machine policies are applied to all managed computers from the time they start and are enforced upon application or file execution. User policies are applied at the user level and are enforced through the duration of a user session upon application or file execution. A Software Restriction Policy consists of a default security level that defines if an application is allowed to run along with the rules that specify exceptions to the default security level.

List 12.2 highlights Software Restriction Policies capabilities:
- Specify which applications are allowed to execute.
- Specify which applications are not allowed to execute.
- Permit only specific file types to execute, such as: MSI, EXE, BAT, COM, ActiveX and VBS.
- Prevent files from running if the computer is infected with a virus.

Note: The implementation of Software Restriction Policies requires extensive testing to ensure that applications function properly and that the user environment is not too restrictive. Each organization should evaluate its unique requirements in order to develop Software Restriction Policies that provide sufficient security and manageability without limiting user productivity.

Software Restriction Policies can be applied in one of two security levels, Unrestricted or Disallowed. The Unrestricted security level is a blacklist policy that allows administrators to specify which application will not execute, and all other applications are allowed. The Disallowed security level is a white-list policy that allows administrators to specify which applications are permitted to execute, and all other applications are restricted. The Disallowed security level provides a higher level of security than Unrestricted because of the ability to restrict access to known trusted applications. One of the two security levels must be selected as the default policy security level.

A number of exceptions to the Disallowed security level require careful consideration while developing policies. For example, setting the security level to Disallowed will not prevent all software from executing on a machine.

List 12.3 highlights Disallowed security level exceptions:
- The default rules insure that when the Disallowed security level is used, and if no applications are defined as Unrestricted, the operating system will still boot.
- Programs that execute with the SYSTEM account will still execute.
- Drivers and supplementary kernel mode software will still execute.
- Programs written for the common language runtime (CLR) are not restricted.
- Microsoft Office 2000 or Office XP Macros are not restricted.

There are two methods to determine which security level to use. If a comprehensive list of approved applications with their associated users has been developed, policies with the Disallowed security level can be created to allow only known trusted applications and files to execute (a white list policy). If no approved application to user list has been created, a policy with the Unrestricted security level can be developed to restrict only un-trusted applications or file types.

Once the default security level is selected, the next step is to create exceptions to the security level that allow or restrict an application to execute. For example, a Software Restriction Policy with the default security level of Unrestricted allows all applications to execute excluding applications that have been configured with exceptions. With this example, the exception to the Unrestricted security level specifies which applications are not allowed to execute. A Software Restriction Policy with the default security level of Disallowed allows exceptions to be created that define which applications are allowed to execute. Implementing the Disallowed security level involves significantly more upfront administrative work to determine exactly which applications are permitted and to test and validate the policy.

Regardless of the default security level, when a policy is created, the administrator must select one of four rules. Each rule uses a different evaluation criterion on the application or file. The four types of rules that can be selected are hash, certificate, path and Internet zone. Each rule uses a different strategy to evaluate if an application can or cannot execute.

It is possible that a file is subjected to more than one rule. When this happens, rules are evaluated in the following order: hash rule, certificate rule, path rule and finally the Internet zone rule. Also rules that more closely match a file will override more general rules.

Hash Rule

While configuring a hash rule, one of the steps is to browse to the location of an application's executable in order to calculate its hash value. A hash is a cryptographic fingerprint of a file that is created using a hash algorithm. The hash is used as a criterion to decide if the file is allowed to execute. When an attempt is made to execute a file, the hash value from the file is compared to the hash value from the rule. If the values match, then the file is processed based on the default security level, such as allowed to execute or not. If the hash values do not match the file, it will be prevented from opening. The hash values detects if a file has been altered in any way, such as from a virus or tampering since the creation of the hash rule.

A hash rule is an effective security control even if an application is renamed or moved because the hash value is based on a cryptographic calculation from the files contents. However, any changes to the application's binary (i.e. updates, rebasing, re-linking, or digital signing) will result in changes in the hash value and the hash rule will no longer work. Hash rules can also be used to control the use of specific versions of an application, such as to deny one version with a known vulnerability to execute while allowing another trusted version to run.

Path rules

A path rule can specify a directory or fully qualified path to an application as the criteria to determine if access is allowed. When a directory is specified, it refers to all applications within that directory and its subdirectories. Path rules can also be used to allow access to network resources, such as shared applications or scripts. Path rules support the use of environment variables, for example %program files%. Because a path rule is specified by its path, if an application is moved, the path rule will no longer apply. Path rules also support registry rules, which are handy security controls to manage what can execute out of registry autostartup locations, like the RunOnce key. The ability to control registry paths that perform autostartup tasks can control malicious code when it tries to install itself on a machine.

Path rules require the use of access control lists (ACLs) to control if code can be accessed and executed. When configuring a directory or a fully qualified path, it is necessary to ensure that the ACLs are properly configured in order to avoid files system permission issues. Note that registry path rules are protected by default by ACLs and use embedded environment variables. Along with the ability to control registry autostartup locations, path rules can be used to prevent files with double extensions to execute. Double extensions are a common way to trick users into opening a virus. Virus writers use double extensions such as "I LOVE YOU.TXT.vbs" which is not a .TXT file, but a .vbs file. A path rule such as "*.???.EXE" will control the execution of code with three letter double extensions. It is important to note that the use of environment variables with path rules introduces risk because any user who can access a command prompt could change the environment variables for the duration of the session.

Certificate Rules

A certificate rule recognizes applications using digital certificates. The digital certificates are used as an evaluation criterion to determine if an application is allowed to execute. Certificate rules only apply to Windows Installer packages (MSI) and scripts that have been digitally signed. The digital certificate can validate if an application's binary has changed since the digital certificate was created. The certificates used for a certificate rule should be supplied from the vendor or developer that developed the code. Certificates can be issued from a commercial or private Certificate Authority (CA).

A certificate rule is an effective security control even if the application is renamed or moved because it uses signed hashes contained in the signature of the signed file. Certificate rules are easier to manage than hash rules because one certificate rule can be used to allow all

180

applications from a single source to be trusted automatically, based on the application's digital signature. For example, an administrator can configure a certificate rule to allow only software signed by Microsoft to be installed. Certificate rules are a useful technique to trust software from a single source without the need to create rules for each individual piece of software.

Internet Zone Rules

An Internet zone rule uses Internet Explorer zones as the criteria to determine if software can be installed. Internet zone rules apply only to Windows Installer format (MSI) files; all other file formats cannot be controlled by Internet zone rules. The five zones are Internet, Intranet, Restricted Sites, Trusted Sites and My Computer.

When an MSI file is download, Internet Explorer determines from which zone the file originated and applies the appropriate security level based on the zone. For example, a policy can be created that allows files to be installed that originate from the Intranet or Trusted Sites zone. Conversely, downloaded MSI files that originate from the Internet or Restricted Sites zone can be restricted from installing.

Software Restriction Policy Planning

Following an established logical process for decision making is the key to ensure that Software Restriction Policies will work. The first step is to specify the requirements and keep them at the forefront of all policy development decisions.

List 12.4 highlights a number of high level planning phase decisions used to develop Software Restriction Policies:

- Will the default security level be Unrestricted or Disallowed?
- Will policies be applied at the user or machine level?
- Will the members of the local administrators' group be affected by the rules?
- Will policies apply to all executables excluding libraries (i.e. dlls)?
- Will specific file extensions be considered executables?
- Will end users, local administrators or enterprise administrators be allowed to determine who is a trusted publisher?

- What will be confirmed before trusting a certificate, its publisher or its timestamp?

By default, Software Restriction Policies use the Unrestricted security level, which allows all software to execute. If a black-list policy is desired, the default security level can be used with the addition of exceptions to prohibit specific applications. If more control and a greater degree of security are required, a white-list policy can be implemented using the Disallowed security level, with exceptions that allow only known trusted applications and restrict everything else.

The default rules insure that when the Disallowed security level is used and no applications are specified as Unrestricted, the operating system will still work. It is possible to configure exceptions to control executables and drivers that reside within the default rules. Another consideration when using the Disallowed security level is how to deal with .dlls. Many applications have dependencies other than their executables, such as .dlls. There are two ways to manage .dlls. One is the default setting which assumes that .dlls are treated like the executable, either allowed or denied. The second option specifies if .dlls are treated as executables that require a rule for each executable and .dll. The latter option offers greater security with substantially higher administrative overhead. The settings are configured from the Enforcement Properties window.

Figure 12.1 shows the Enforcement Properties window.

Figure 12.1

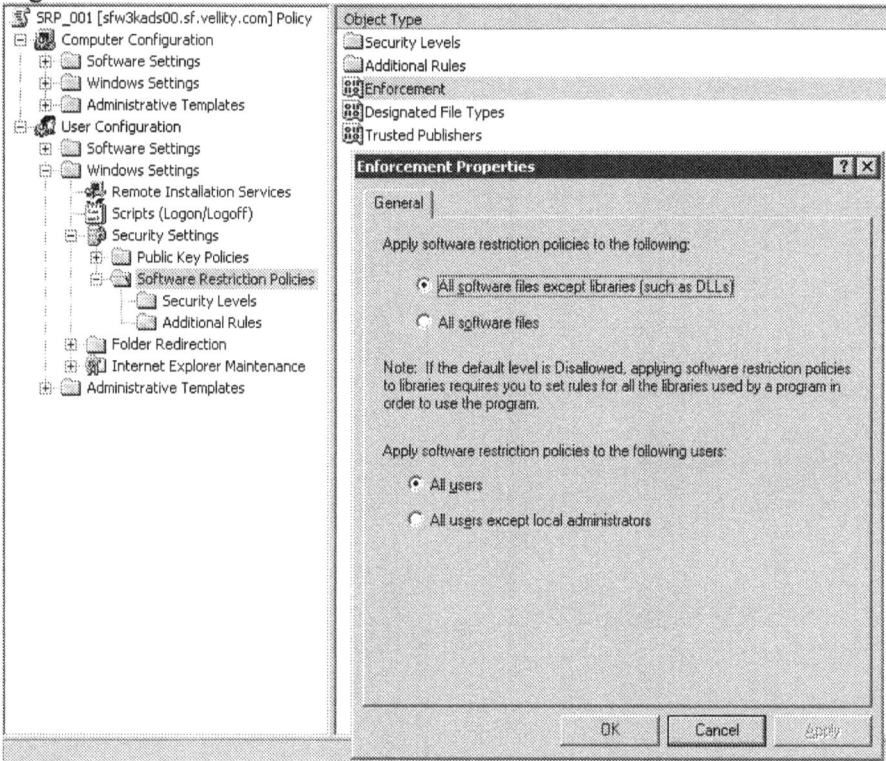

Software Restriction Policies allow the configuration of designated file types to specify what an executable is, such as .exe, .dll, and .vbs. File types can be added or removed from the default list by accessing the Designated File Types properties window as shown in Figure 12.2. It is important to update the file type list routinely with new, executable file types to ensure they are secured. For example, if the security level is set to Disallowed and an attempt to execute an unlisted executable is made, the executable will run! Therefore, as new applications are placed into production or new vulnerabilities are identified, it is important to add the file types to the list.

Figure 12.2

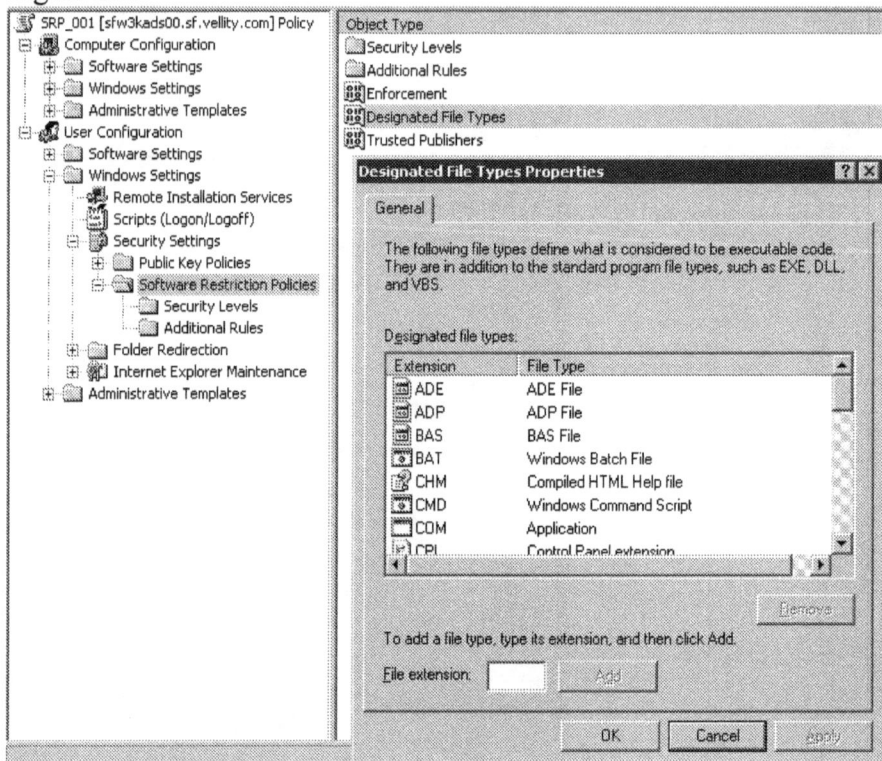

Software Restriction Policies Best Practices

List 12.5 highlights Software Restriction Policies best practices:

- Consider creating a separate Group Policy Object for each Software Restriction Policy. From a testing and operations perspective, this policy provides the flexibility to disable a specific Software Restriction Policy Group Policy Object without affecting any other Group policy settings.

- While developing policies it is possible to lock yourself and all users out of the machine. A quick way to circumvent Software Restriction Policies is to reboot the machine into safe mode. While in safe mode, policies are not applied and administrative capabilities will be restored. Edit the policy, execute "gpupdate", and then restart the computer.

- The implementation of Software Restriction Policies requires extensive testing before being placed into production to ensure that applications function properly and that the user environment is not too restrictive.

The next section will introduce an example Software Restriction Policy Baseline. It begins with a Purpose and Scope statement and then proceeds with the procedure to configure a Software Restriction Policy. It concludes with a Policy Review and Compliance statement. This baseline is intended for informational purposes only.

Software Restriction Policy Baseline

Purpose:

The purpose of this baseline is to define standards for the configuration of Microsoft Software Restriction Policies. Software Restriction Policies provide the security controls needed to manage application and file execution entitlements as well as the ability to mitigate the introduction of hostile code through email or web browsing. Before any servers are placed on the production network, standard processes will be executed to ensure that all servers are installed and maintained in a manner that prevents unauthorized access, unauthorized use and disruptions in service.

Scope:

This baseline is intended for all Windows Terminal Servers on the internal network and will be reviewed in conjunction with the other IT infrastructure policies.

Baseline:

The following procedure will create a test Group Policy Object linked to the WTS Organizational Unit. The Group Policy Object will be created, tested and validated in a lab or pilot environment on a test server. The test server will be provisioned identically as the production Terminal Servers. The Group Policy Object settings will be validated with non-administrative and administrative user accounts. While testing the Group Policy Object, the revision number will be appended to the end of the file name, such as. SRP_DEV01, SRP_DEV02, and so forth. After a Group Policy Object is validated, it will be named SRP_Prod_month/day/year and placed in production. Group Policy

Object configurations will be made using the Group Policy Management Console.

1 Log on to a domain member server as administrator that has the Group Policy Management Console.

2 From the server desktop, click **Start** and then click **Run**, type "gpmc.msc /a." Next, press **Enter** to access the Group Policy Management Console.

3 From the Group Policy Management console in the left pane, expand the "forest and domain" nodes and select the "WTS Organizational Unit." Right click the "WTS Organizational Unit." From the dialogue menu, click the "Create and link a GPO here" option.

4 From the New GPO window enter the name of the GPO, such as. "SRP_DEV01." Click **OK** to proceed.

5 Once the Group Policy Management Console refreshes the new Group Policy Object will be listed under the WTS OU. Select the new Group Policy Object and right click it. From the dialogue menu select **Edit** to access its properties.

6 Navigate to the User Configuration > Windows Settings > Security Settings > Software Restriction Policies node. Right click the node and select the "New Software Restriction Policies" option.

7 Select the "Security Levels" node. Double click the "Disallowed security level." From the Disallowed properties window, click the **Set** as default button. When presented with the Software Restriction Policies informational window, click **Yes** and then **OK** to close the Disallowed properties window.

8 Select and right click the "Additional Rules" node. Select the "New Hash Rule" option.

9 From the New Hash Rule properties window, click the **Browse** button and browse to the desired executable.

10 A hash value will be created, next set the Security Level to "Unrestricted." Click **OK** to close the New Hash Rule properties window.

11 Close the Group Policy Object window and the Group Policy Management Console.

Policy Review
This policy will be reviewed quarterly.

Compliance
Any employee found to have violated this policy may be subject to disciplinary action, up to and including termination of employment.

Chapter 12 Summary
This chapter began with an overview of why organizations implement application access restrictions, then introduced Microsoft Software Restriction Policies and concluded with an example tier 3 Software Restriction Policy Baseline.

- Providing users with full access to their computer results in policy violations, system and security issues and results in an increased number of help desk calls, licensing violations and data loss.
- Implementing security controls that limit user access rights to computers shores up an organization's security posture by mitigating accidental or deliberate damage to computers, applications and data.
- Organizations turn to desktop security and application access restrictions to manage user access rights on computers.
- The default behavior with Terminal Server is to assume that all legitimate users have access to all applications installed on a Terminal Server.
- There are two strategies used to implement application restrictions, a black-list or white-list policy.
- Microsoft Software Restriction Policies provides an integrated framework to implement granular application and file execution rules using Active Directory Group Policy without the need of any additional 3rd party software.
- Software Restriction Policies provides the security controls to manage application and file execution rules as well as the ability to mitigate the introduction of hostile code through email or web browsing, such as script based viruses or Active X controls.

- Software Restriction Policies are created using the Group Policy Management Console and can be applied to local machines, sites, domains or Organizational Units.
- Software Restriction Policies can be applied in one of two security levels: Unrestricted or Disallowed.
- There are a number of exceptions to the Disallowed security level that require consideration in developing policies.
- Regardless of the default security level, when a policy is created, the administrator must select one of four rules: hash, certificate, path or Internet zone.
- It is possible that a file is subjected to more than one rule. When a file is subjected to more than one rule, rules are evaluated in the following order: hash rule, certificate rule, path rule and finally the Internet zone rule.
- Following an established logical process for decision making is the key to ensure that Software Restriction Policies will work. The first step is to specify the requirements and keep them at the forefront of all policy development decisions.
- By default, Software Restriction Policies use the Unrestricted security level which allows all software to execute.
- While developing policies, it is possible to lock yourself and all users out of the machine. A quick way to circumvent Software Restriction Policies is to reboot the machine into safe mode. While in safe mode, policies are not applied and administrative capabilities will be restored.
- The implementation of Software Restriction Policies requires extensive testing before being placed into production to ensure that applications function properly and that the user environment is not too restrictive.

The next chapter will review Microsoft Session Directory functionality and introduces two tier 3 Session Directory Configuration Baselines.

Chapter 13: Session Directory Configuration Baseline

Chapter Overview:

This chapter will review two tier 3 Session Directory Configuration Baselines. The first baseline is a Session Directory Configuration Baseline that specifies an organization's approved installation and configuration standard for Microsoft Session Directory. It is followed by a Terminal Server Session Directory Group Policy Configuration Baseline that defines an approved configuration standard for Terminal Servers that participate in a Terminal Server Session Directory.

Organizations develop baseline configurations to introduce Quality Assurance (QA) and reduce risk associated with the installation and configuration of technologies. Baselines are security controls that work in conjunction with other security controls, such as policies and standards. Together these policies provide guidance to plan, build, run and monitor an organization's technology portfolio as a single unit.

As discussed in Chapter 2, it is important to consider what happens when the Session Directory fails. Other than losing Session Directory functionality, logon times will increase because each Terminal Server attempts to connect to the unavailable Session Directory server. With large server farms, a failed Session Directory can affect the availability of services. Microsoft clustering technology can be implemented to provide fault tolerance and high availability for the Session Directory to help meet business and regulatory requirements.

From a regulatory compliance perspective, Session Directory fault tolerance is often a requirement. A Risk Assessment should be conducted to validate whether regulatory or business requirements mandate Session Directory fault tolerance.

To use the Session Directory, the following three configurations are needed:

1. Turn on the Session Directory service. (Session Directory Server)
2. Add each Terminal Server account to the Session Directory Computers group. (Session Directory Server)
3. Configure each Windows Server 2003 Enterprise Edition Terminal Server in the farm to participate in the Session Directory. (Terminal Servers)

The first two configurations are made locally on the server hosting the Session Directory service. The third configuration can be made in one of three ways: locally on each server with local Server Policy, locally on each server with the Terminal Services Configuration Tool (tscc.msc), or centrally via Active Directory Group Policy. Each option has its pros and cons. Microsoft recommends using Active Directory because it is configured and managed centrally. Business requirements and personal preference will dictate the configuration used for an environment.

As discussed in Chapter 2, the first time the Session Directory service is started, a new local group is created called Session Directory Computers. By default, the Session Directory Computers group is empty. Access to Session Directory functionality must be explicitly granted by adding each Terminal Server's domain computer account to the Session Directory group. The Session Directory service will only accept connections from servers in this local group. The accounts can be added individually or by creating a domain group containing the Terminal Servers and then adding the domain group to the local Session Directory Computers group.

List 13.1 shows the prerequisites and assumptions for the following Session Directory Configuration Baseline:

*   The domain member server hosting the Session Directory service is on a highly-available hardware platform.
*   Terminal Server domain computer accounts have been added to a domain group that will be added to the Session Directory Computers group.

190

The following example Session Directory Configuration Baseline reviews the configuration of a single member server in an Active Directory domain supporting a load-balanced Terminal Server farm. The example baseline begins with a Purpose and Scope statement and then continues with the procedure to turn on the Session Directory service. It concludes with adding a domain group that contains the Terminal Server farm members. This baseline is intended for informational purposes only.

Session Directory Configuration Baseline

Purpose
The purpose of this baseline is to define standards for the installation and baseline configuration of Microsoft Session Directory. Before any servers are placed on the production network, standard processes will be executed to ensure that all servers are installed and maintained in a manner that prevents unauthorized access, unauthorized use and disruptions in service.

Scope
This baseline is for all Windows Session Directory servers on the internal network and will be reviewed in conjunction with the other IT infrastructure policies.

Baseline
Part 1: Turn on the Session Directory Service
1. Log on to the Session Directory server as administrator.
2. From the Session Directory server desktop, click **Start**, click **Run**, type "services.msc /a," and then press **Enter** to access the Services Console.
3. As shown in figure 1, from the right pane under the Name column, double click the "Terminal Services Session Directory" service to access its properties.

Figure 1

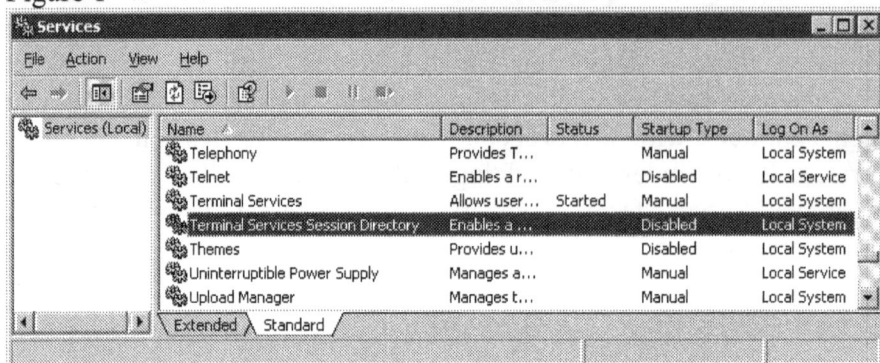

4. From Terminal Services Session Directory Properties General tab, change the Start up type from Disabled to Automatic, and then click **Apply**. Next click the **Start** button to start the Session Directory service. Validate that the service status is Started to proceed.

5. As shown in Figure 2, from the Services Console, validate that the Terminal Services Session Directory service is Started and the Startup Type is set to Automatic. Close the Services Console.

Figure 2

Name	Description	Status	Startup Type
Terminal Services Session Directory	Enables a ...	Started	Automatic

Configuration Baseline
Part 2: Add the domain group with the Terminal Server domain computer accounts to the Session Directory Computers group.

1. From the Session Directory server desktop, click **Start**, click **Run**, type "lusrmgr.msc /a," and then press **Enter** to access the Local Users and Groups Console.

2. As shown in figure 3, in the left pane of the tree view select "Groups" and then in the right pane double click the "Session Directory Computers" group to access its properties.

Figure 3

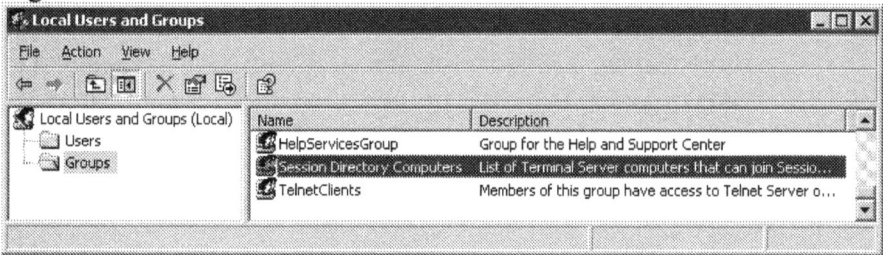

3. From the Session Directory Computers properties, click **Add** to access the Select Users, Computers, or Groups window.
4. Click the "Object Types" button. From the Object Types window, select the Computers node and click **OK**.
5. Enter the name of the Terminal Server domain group in the "Enter the object name to select" text box. Then click the "Check Names" button to validate the name of the Terminal Server domain group. After the name of the Group is validated, click **OK** to complete the procedure.

Policy Review
This policy will be reviewed annually.

Compliance
Any employee found to have violated this policy may be subject to disciplinary action, up to and including termination of employment.

Related Policies, Standards, and Guidelines
Change Management Policy

The next example is a Terminal Server Session Directory Group Policy Configuration Baseline.

List 13.2 shows prerequisites and assumptions for the following Terminal Server Session Directory Group Policy Configuration Baseline:
- The Group Policy Management Console is available on the target domain member server.

- All Terminal Server computer objects are in an Organizational Unit (OU) named WTS (Windows Terminal Server).
- Terminal Server domain computer accounts have been added to a domain group that will be added to the Session Directory Computers group.

Terminal Server Session Directory Group Policy Configuration Baseline

Purpose
The purpose of this policy is to define standards for the baseline configuration of <Company Name>'s Windows Terminal Servers that participate in the Terminal Server Session Directory. Before any servers are placed on the production network, standard processes will be executed to ensure that all servers are installed and maintained in a manner that prevents unauthorized access, unauthorized use and disruptions in service.

Scope
This policy is specifically for all Windows Terminal Servers that participate in the Terminal Server Session Directory on the internal network.

Configuration Baseline
Group Policy Configuration
1. Log on to a domain member server as administrator. From the desktop, click **Start**, click **Run**, type "gpmc.msc /a," and then press **Enter** to access the Group Policy Management Console.
2. In the left pane of the tree view, expand the Terminal Server OU. Select and right click the "WTS_Prod_month/day/year" Group Policy Object and click **Edit**.
3. In the left pane of the tree view node, navigate to Computer Configuration > Administrative Templates > Windows Components > Terminal Services > Session Directory. Double-click the "Session Directory Server" policy to access its properties.
4. From the Session Directory Server Properties' Settings tab, change the setting from "Not Configured" to "Enabled" and then type the "FQDN" of the server hosting the Terminal Services Session

directory service in the "Session Directory Server" text box. Click **OK** to save the settings and close the window.

5. Double click the "Session Directory Cluster Name" Setting to configure its properties.
6. From the Session Directory Cluster Name Properties' Settings tab change the setting from "Not Configured" to "Enabled." Then type the "FQDN" of the Session Directory Cluster Name in the "Session Directory Cluster Name" text box. Click **OK** to save the settings and close the window.
7. From the Group Policy Object Editor Console, double click the "Join Session Directory Setting" to access its properties.
8. From the Join Session Directory's Settings tab, change the setting from "Not Configured" to "Enabled." Click **OK** to save the settings and close the window.
9. From the Group Policy Object Editor console, validate that the state of the Join Session Directory, Session Directory Server, and Session Directory Cluster Name settings are Enabled.
10. Close the Group Policy Object Editor console and the Group Policy Management Console to conclude the procedure.

Policy Review
This policy will be reviewed annually.

Compliance
Any employee found to have violated this policy may be subject to disciplinary action, up to and including termination of employment.

Related Policies, Standards, and Guidelines
Change Management Policy

Chapter 13 Summary
This chapter began with a review of a baseline policies followed by an overview of the Session Directory feature, Session Directory design considerations, and required Session Directory configurations. This chapter concluded with two example baselines: Session Directory Configuration Baseline and Terminal Server Session Directory Group Policy Configuration Baseline.

- Baseline configurations introduce Quality Assurance (QA) and reduce risk associated with the installation and configuration of technologies.
- Baselines are security controls that work in conjunction with other security controls, such as Policies and Standards.
- A Session Directory Configuration Baseline defines the approved installation and configuration standards for Microsoft's Session Directory.
- A Terminal Server Session Directory Group Policy Configuration Baseline is used to define an approved configuration standard for Terminal Servers that participate in a Terminal Server Session Directory environment.
- From a regulatory compliance perspective, Session Directory fault tolerance is often a requirement. A Risk Assessment should be conducted to validate if regulatory or business requirements mandate Session Directory fault tolerance.
- To use the Session Directory three configurations are needed.

The next chapter will review Microsoft's Network Load-Balancing technology and introduce a tier 3 Terminal Server Network Load-Balancing Configuration Baseline.

Chapter 14: Terminal Server Network Load-Balancing Baseline

Chapter Overview:

This chapter begins with a brief overview of a Terminal Server Network Load-Balancing Baseline and then reviews Microsoft's Network Load-Balancing technology. The chapter concludes with an example Terminal Server Network Load-Balancing Baseline.

A Terminal Server Network Load-Balancing Baseline defines an organization's approved installation and configuration standards for Microsoft's Network Load-Balancing for Terminal Servers. It is used by employees as an approved procedure to implement Load-Balancing in a Terminal Server environment.

Microsoft first released Network Load-Balancing (NLB) with Windows 2000 Server Enterprise edition. In the present day, it is included with each edition of Windows 2003 Server. Network Load-Balancing allows a group of servers to be configured as a load-balanced cluster with a single Virtual IP address (VIP). Users access the cluster with the DNS name associated with the Virtual IP address. All machines in the cluster respond in sequence to requests from the Virtual IP address and re-route the request to one of the servers in the Load-Balanced cluster. Network Load-Balancing provides high availability for a Terminal Server environment by evenly distributing user load across a Terminal Server farm. If a server in the cluster becomes unavailable, Network Load-Balancing will detect the unavailable server and direct new user connections to an available server in the cluster.

In order to set-up Network Load-Balancing, a minimum of two servers running Windows Server 2003 is required. Each server needs at least one network card and a single fixed IP address. Although using one adapter will work, for optimum performance Microsoft recommends two network adapters in each server: one network adapter mapped to the real IP Address and one mapped to the Virtual IP address.

List 14.1 shows the prerequisites and assumptions for the following Terminal Server Network Load-Balancing Configuration Baseline:
- An available Virtual IP address for the load-balanced cluster.
- The load-balanced cluster cannot exceed 32 servers. (NLB limit is 32 servers)
- All servers must be on the same subnet.
- Each server will have a fixed IP address and at least one network adapter.

This next section will review the Load-Balancing cluster properties and provide an understanding of each setting used in the example baseline.

1. A virtual IP address, subnet mask and the DNS cluster name.
2. Decide between unicast or multicast cluster operation mode.
   - With unicast mode, Network Load-Balancing replaces the network card's original MAC address.
   - With multicast mode, Network Load-Balancing adds the new virtual MAC to the network card and retains the network card's original MAC address.
Note: Use unicast only if the Terminal Servers have two network cards and multicast mode if there is only one network adapter.
3. Remote Control. Remote Control allows centralized management of a load-balanced cluster. Microsoft recommends not enabling Remote Control because it exposes known vulnerabilities to a cluster. If remote control is enabled, it is important to firewall the cluster to isolate the User Datagram Protocol (UDP) ports that facilitate the remote-control commands. By default, these are ports 1717 and 2504 at the cluster IP address.
4. Host Parameters. The Host Priority identifier is a unique number assigned to each host in the cluster.
5. Port Rules allows the configuration of how load-balancing works within the cluster. For a Terminal Server cluster, the setting will need to be changed from default.

- The Affinity setting controls how all TCP connections from one client IP address connects to the same cluster host. Applications like Terminal Server that maintain session state are considered stateful. Stateful applications require affinity with the cluster host when the session state is maintained locally.

The following Network Load-Balancing Configuration Baseline will show the procedure to configure Network Load-Balancing for a single Terminal Server. The procedure needs to be executed on each Terminal Server in the Load-Balanced cluster. The example baseline starts with a Purpose and Scope statement and then proceeds with the baseline configurations. This baseline is intended for informational purposes only.

Terminal Server Network Load-Balancing Configuration Baseline

Purpose
The purpose of this baseline is to define standards for the installation and baseline configuration of Microsoft Network Load-Balancing for Terminal Servers. Before any servers are placed on the production network, standard processes will be executed to ensure that all servers are installed and maintained in a manner that prevents unauthorized access, unauthorized use and disruptions in service.

Scope
This baseline is specifically for all Windows Terminal Servers in a load-balanced cluster on the internal network and will be reviewed in conjunction with the other IT infrastructure policies.

Configuration Baseline
Part 1. Create the Cluster
1. Log on to the target Terminal Server as administrator. This server will be the first server in the cluster.
Note: This procedure will need to be executed on each Terminal Server in the cluster.

2. From the Terminal Server desktop, click **Start**, click **Run**, type "nlbmgr.exe," and then press **Enter** to access the Network Load-Balancing console.

3. As shown in figure 1, in the left pane of the tree view, highlight the "Network Load Balance Clusters" node, right click it, and click the "New Cluster" menu item.

Figure 1

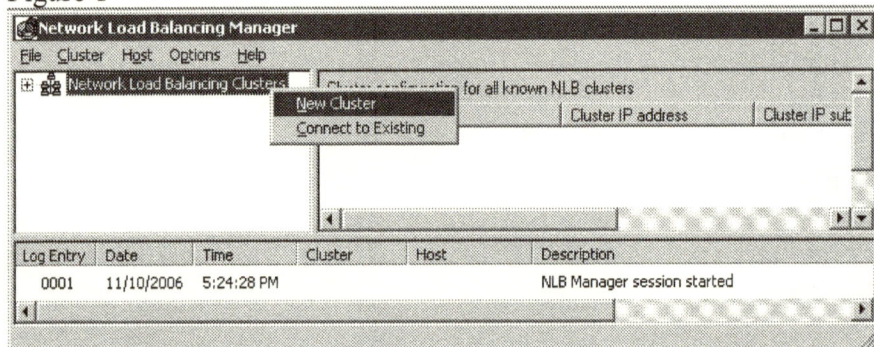

4. From the Cluster Parameters window enter the "IP address" of the cluster (Virtual IP address), "subnet mask", the "Full Internet Name" (the DNS name associated with the Virtual IP address), and select "Multicast." **Note:** Do not enable remote control. Click **Next** to proceed.

5. From the Cluster IP Address window click **Next** to proceed.

6. From the Port Rules window highlight the default port rule and click **Edit** to proceed.

7. As shown in Figure 2, in the Port range section, enter "3389" in the From and To area. In the Protocol section, select the "TCP" radio button. In the Filtering mode area, select the "Multiple host" radio button. Click **OK** to proceed.

Figure 2

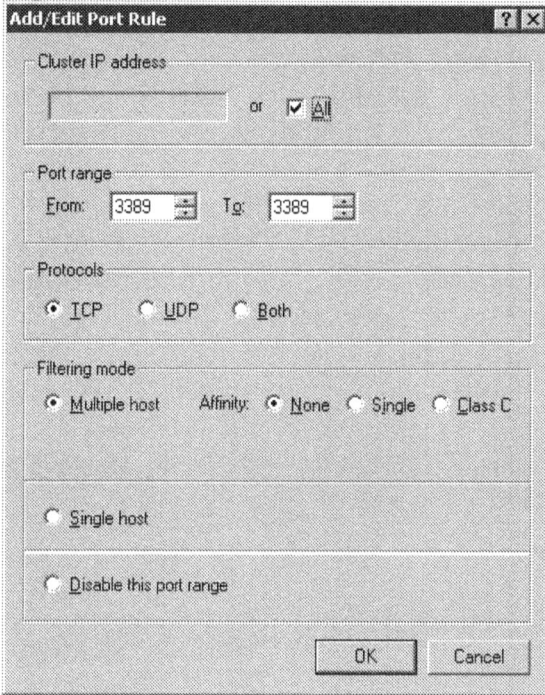

8. From the Port Rules window, click **Next** to proceed.
9. From the connect window, enter the "FQDN" of the first server in the cluster in the Host text box and click connect. Once connected, the server will appear in the "Interfaces available for configuring a new cluster" area. Highlight the interface and click **Next** to proceed.
10. From the Host parameters window, enter the "IP address" and "subnet mask" of the Terminal Server. Accept the other defaults and click **Finish** to proceed.
11. As shown in Figure 3, the new cluster will be displayed.

Figure 3

Configuration Baseline
Part 2, Add a Host to the Cluster

1. To add a host to the cluster, log on to the target Terminal Server as administrator. From the server desktop, click **Start**, click **Run**, type "nlbmgr.exe," and then press **Enter** to access the Network Load Balancing Console. In the left pane of the tree view, highlight the Network Load Balancing Cluster node and click the "Connect to Existing" menu option.

2. From the connect window, enter the "FQDN" of a server in the cluster in the Host text box and click connect. Once connected, the server will appear in the "Interfaces available for configuring a new cluster" area. Highlight the interface and click **Next** to proceed.

3. The cluster will be displayed in the Network Load Balancing Console, as shown in Figure 4.

Figure 4

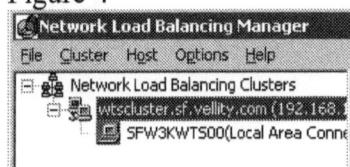

4. As shown in Figure 5, in the left pane of the tree view, highlight and right click the cluster. From the menu click the "Add Host To Cluster" menu option.

Figure 5

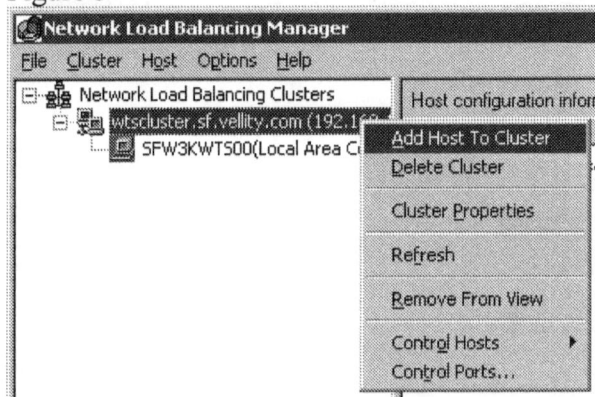

5. From the Connect window, enter the "NetBIOS" or "FQDN" of the desired Terminal Server in the Host text box and click the **Connect** button. Once the Terminal Server is discovered, highlight it and click **Next** to proceed.
6. From the Host parameters window, enter the "IP address" and "subnet mask" of target Terminal Server. Click **Finish** to proceed. Note that the Priority number should automatically increment.
7. As shown in Figure 6 the additional Terminal Server has been added to the cluster and the configurations have been saved.

Figure 6

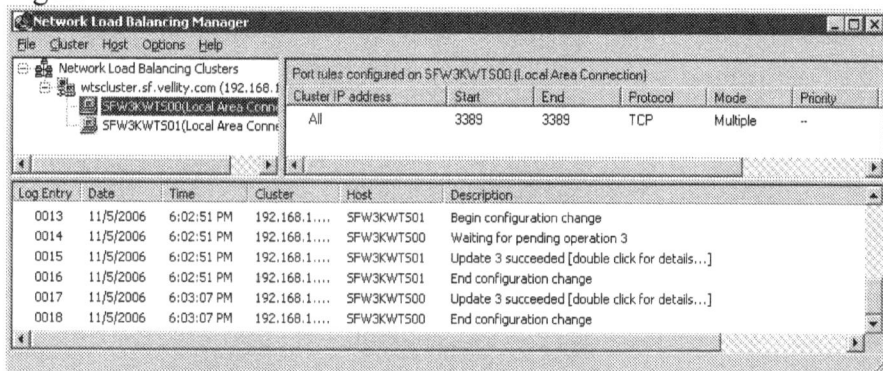

8. Exit the Network Load Balancing Console and log off the server.

Policy Review
This policy will be reviewed annually.

Compliance
Any employee found to have violated this policy may be subject to disciplinary action, up to and including termination of employment.

Related Policies, Standards, and Guidelines
Change Management Policy

Chapter 14 Summary
This chapter discussed Network Load-Balancing followed with a Network Load-Balancing Configuration Baseline.

- A Terminal Server Network Load-Balancing Baseline defines the installation and configuration standards for Microsoft's Network Load-Balancing for Terminal Servers.
- Network Load-Balancing (NLB) is included with each edition of Windows 2003 Server.
- The minimum requirement for Network Load-Balancing is two servers running Windows Server 2003. Each server needs at least one network card and a single fixed IP address.
- Network Load-Balancing allows a group of servers to be configured as a load-balanced cluster accessed with a single Virtual IP address (VIP).
- Network Load-Balancing provides high availability for a Terminal Server environment by evenly distributing user load across a Terminal Server farm.
- If a server in the cluster becomes unavailable, Network Load-Balancing will detect the unavailable server and direct new user connections to an available server in the cluster.

The next chapter will introduce system auditing and security monitoring a Terminal Server environment.

Chapter 15: Terminal Server System Auditing

Chapter Overview:
This chapter introduces Terminal Server System Auditing strategies using Microsoft Baseline Security Analyzer and Nmap. The goal of this chapter is to introduce security auditing strategies for Terminal Server while providing direction to satisfy information security and regulatory mandates.

Pre- and Post-Production Auditing

All production servers should undergo regular security audits to ensure compliance with security policies and regulatory mandates. Pre- and post-production audits validate that a server is configured to specifications, eliminating possible security holes and missing hotfixes or patches. All servers should undergo pre-production audits whereas the frequency of production audits depends on business and regulatory requirements.

The following sections will introduce system auditing using Microsoft Baseline Security Analyzer (MBSA) and Nmap. We will walk through how to execute a scan against a Terminal Server then analyze and compare the results against security policies. Although there are countless commercial and Open Source auditing and scanning solutions, I selected Microsoft Baseline Security Analyzer and Nmap because of their performance, price (they are both free) and widespread industry adoption.

The next section will introduce Microsoft Baseline Security Analyzer and follow with an example scan.

Microsoft Baseline Security Analyzer

Microsoft Baseline Security Analyzer is part of the Microsoft trustworthy computing initiative. It is a tool to help determine the security posture of Windows servers and many other Microsoft products. The results from a Microsoft Baseline Security Analyzer scan include Microsoft's security recommendations and presents detailed remediation steps. Microsoft Baseline Security Analyzer is built on the Windows Update Agent and Microsoft Update infrastructure and supports Windows NT 4.0 SP4 or above, Windows 2000, Windows XP, Windows Server 2003, IIS 4.0 or above, SQL 7.0 and above, and Office 2000 and above. To run the Microsoft Baseline Security Analyzer, you must have local administrator rights to the computer you want to scan. Remote scans will require the Remote Registry service to be enabled.

Note: The Terminal Server Security Baseline from Chapter 11 explicitly disabled the Remote Registry for security reasons. To enable remote administration while configuring the Server Role with the Security Configuration Wizard, enable Remote Windows Administration from the Select Administration and Other Options screen. The registry setting is located:
[HKEY_LOCAL_MACHINE\SYSTEM\CurrentControlSet\Services\RemoteRegistry]
The "Start" dword controls the start up type. 00000002 is automatic, 00000003 is manual, and 00000004 is disable.

List 15.1 shows the prerequisites and assumptions to use Microsoft Baseline Security Analyzer.
- The Microsoft Baseline Security Analyzer is installed on each host and restrictive application access rights are configured to limit access exclusively to the administrator's group.
- If remote scanning is required, the Remote Registry service will be enabled.
- Servers will be scanned before they are placed into production and at regular intervals governed by policy.

The next example walks through executing a scan on a Terminal Server, followed by an explanation of how to validate the scan against a security policy.

Please Note: Never run scanners without explicit permission (preferably written) from your employer. Auditors and network and security administrators with the best intentions have been fired for running scanners without the proper authority to do so.

1- Log on to the host and run the executable, which by default is installed to "C:\Program Files\Microsoft Baseline Security Analyzer 2\mbsa.exe." You will see the "Welcome to the Microsoft Baseline Security Analyzer" screen as shown in Figure 15.1.

Figure 15.1

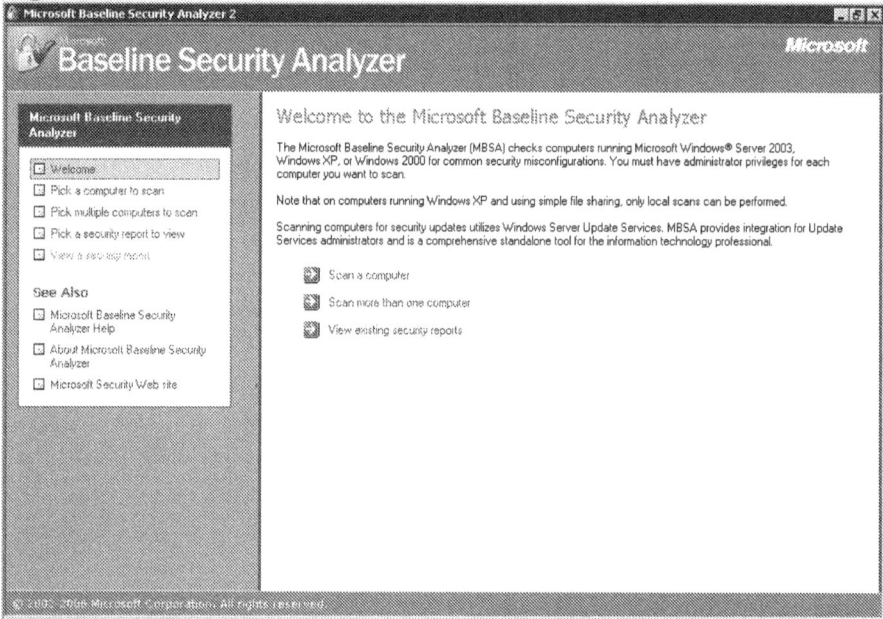

From the welcome screen you can select "Scan a computer", "Scan more than one computer", or "View your existing reports" from computers you have scanned in the past. In this example, click the "Scan a single computer" option to proceed.

Figure 15.2 shows the "Pick a computer to Scan" screen.

Figure 15.2

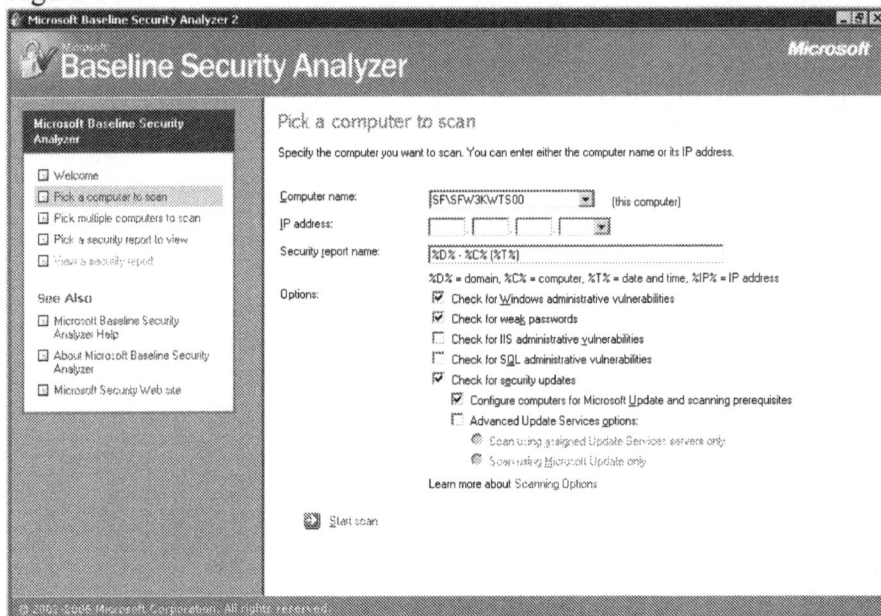

2- From the "Pick a computer to scan" screen, ensure that the computer name is selected in the "Computer name" text box. Accept the default setting for the report name and select the following options:

- Check for Windows administrative vulnerabilities
- Check for Weak Passwords
- Check for security updates
- Configure computers for Microsoft Update and scanning prerequisites

Once you make the selections, click "Start Scan."

List 15.2 lists the security settings that Microsoft Baseline Security Analyzer checks. If a product is not installed on the host that is being scanned, the related product checks will not be run or reported.

Windows checks
- Check for account password expiration.
- Check for file system type on hard drives.
- Check if Auto Logon feature is enabled.
- Check if Guest account is enabled.

- Check the RestrictAnonymous registry key settings.
- Check the number of local Administrator accounts.
- Check for blank or simple local user account passwords.
- Check if unnecessary services are running.
- List the shares present on the computer.
- Check if Windows auditing is enabled.
- Check the Windows version running on the scanned computer.
- Check if Internet Connection Firewall is enabled.
- Check if Automatic Updates is enabled.
- Check if incomplete updates require the computer to be restarted.

IIS checks
- Check if the IIS Lockdown tool (version 2.1) was run on the computer.
- Check if IIS sample applications are installed.
- Check if IIS parent paths are enabled.
- Check if the IIS Admin virtual folder is installed.
- Check if the MSADC and Scripts virtual directories are installed.
- Check if IIS logging is enabled.
- Check if IIS is running on a domain controller.

SQL Server checks
- Check if Administrator's group belongs in Sysadmin role.
- Check if CmdExec role is restricted to Sysadmin only.
- Check if SQL Server is running on a domain controller.
- Check if sa account password is exposed.
- Check SQL Server installation folders access permissions.
- Check if Guest account has database access.
- Check if Everyone group has access to SQL Server registry keys.
- Check if SQL Server service accounts are members of the local Administrators group.
- Check if SQL Server accounts have blank or simple passwords.
- Check the SQL Server authentication mode type.
- Check the number of Sysadmin role members.

Desktop application checks

- List the Internet Explorer security zone settings for each local user.
- Check if Internet Explorer Enhanced Security Configuration is enabled for Administrators.
- Check if Internet Explorer Enhanced Security Configuration is enabled for non-Administrators.
- List the Office products security zone settings for each local user.

Security update checks

- Scan computers for security updates, update rollups and service packs published to Microsoft Update.

After the scan is complete, a summary page will appear as shown in Figure 15.3.

Figure 15.3

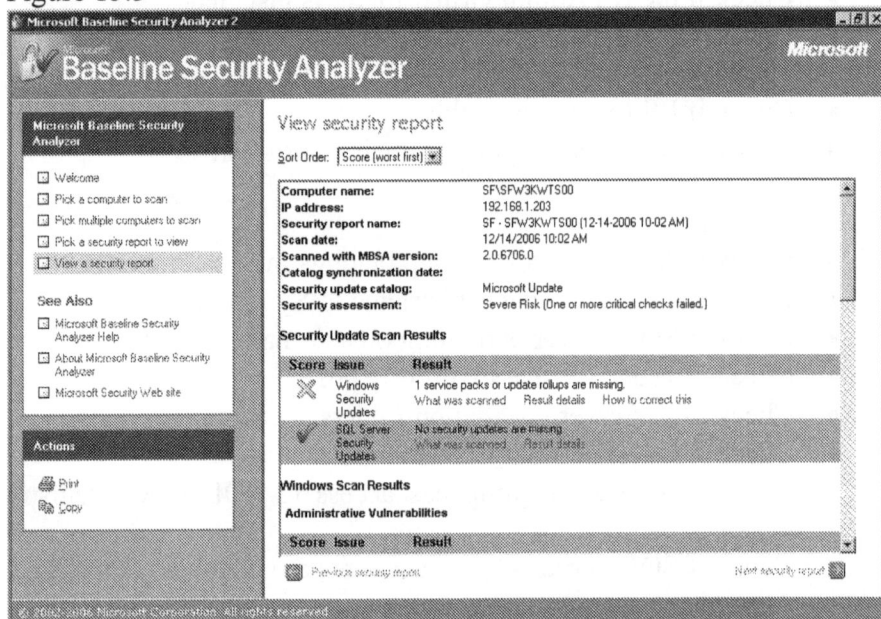

On the View security report screen, vulnerabilities are grouped under one of six categories. List 15.3 shows the categories from the example scan:

- Security Update Scan Results
- Windows Scan Results/Administrative Vulnerabilities.
- Additional System Information.
- Desktop Application Scan Results/Administrative Vulnerabilities.

Each vulnerability is displayed under its respective category with its score, issue and result. There are a total of five scores: Check Failed (Critical), Check Failed (None-critical), Check passed, Additional Information and Best practice.

Figure 15.4 shows the five score images with its explanation.

Figure 15.4

(i) Additional Information

Best practice

Check passed

X Check Failed (Critical)

Check Failed (None-critical)

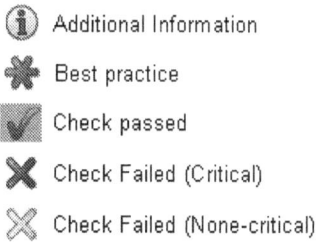

The issue section defines the topic of each vulnerability. The result section includes an explanation of the scan and, in many cases, links to additional information and remediation steps.

The View Security Report page allows us to view, print or copy the summary to compare and analyze it against our Enterprise Architecture security policies. If the analysis validates policy compliance, there are no further steps to be made. If the scan analysis shows discrepancies between the scan summary and our security policies, the policies should define how to remediate the deficiencies, such as repair locally on the host or via Group Policy. After the deficiencies have been fixed, rerun the Microsoft Baseline Security Analyzer to validate policy compliance.

By default the Microsoft Baseline Security Analyzer stores the summary data in the "%userprofile%\SecurityScans" directory. Each time a scan is executed a report with a time stamp is saved in the "%userprofile%\SecurityScans" directory. Reports can be viewed in the Microsoft Baseline Security Analyzer by double clicking the desired file. If a report needs to be deleted, it must be done using Windows Explorer.

Resources
Microsoft   Baseline   Security   Analyzer   Download:
http://www.microsoft.com/technet/security/tools/mbsahome.mspx

The next section will provide an introduction to port scanning and TCP/IP stack fingerprinting with Nmap and present one example scan executed against a Terminal Server to audit it for compliance.

Port Scanning Techniques
This section begins with an introduction of port scanning and port scanning techniques, followed with a review of Nmap. It concludes with an example scan executed against a Terminal Server to audit it for compliance. This section shows how port scanning with Nmap can assist to quickly audit the configuration of a Terminal Server.

Scanners are essential tools for auditors, security and network administrators to quickly determine if a host is running and which services it offers. Scanning software allows us to scan a single machine or an entire network showing which hosts are running, their respected operating systems and what ports they are listening on. For example, let's say a port scan revealed that a machine is listening on port 3389. An intruder knows that it is Terminal Services and could craft an attack against a known Terminal Services vulnerability. Scanning allows us to quickly audit network gear and servers in terms of their respected roles to validate if they are properly configured.

Discovering open ports does not entirely indicate what services are listening and active as illustrated in the example scan. Port numbers range from 0 to 65535 and are separated into three categories: Well Known Ports, Registered Ports, and Dynamic and/or Private Ports. The Well Known Ports range from 0 through 1023. If one or more of these ports are found open, it indicates the assigned service(s) is listening. Registered Ports range from 1024-49151 and Dynamic and/or Private Ports range from 49152 through 65535. Well Known Ports 0 through 1023 are well defined and static in contrast to ports 1024 through 65535 which in some circumstances vary. Registered Ports sometimes vary because many services rely on remote procedure calls (RPC) or Distributed COM (DCOM) features in Windows to assign them dynamic TCP ports. Dynamic TCP port assignment is commonly referred to as random RPC ports.

The assignment of ports is managed by a U. S. association named Intermodal Association of North America (IANA). The port assignment list is a set of recommended ports that is largely followed by the vendors and developers. Quite often vendors or developers select ports for different applications or protocols other than their official IANA designation. This, along with random RPC ports, emphasizes the importance to select a reliable scanner and to thoroughly understand port scanning analysis.

Port scanning techniques have become very sophisticated. Scanning software allows us to create and transmit basic TCP/IP packets and sequences and unusual TCP/IP packets and sequences. Basic scanning techniques are logged by the remote host and can be easily identified by an Intrusion Detection System (IDS). Stealth scanning techniques allow us to craft unusual TCP/IP packets and sequences that can go undetected on a remote system or by an Intrusion Detection System.

With a basic scan, an operating system uses a TCP connect() call to attempt to initiate a TCP connection to a specific port on a remote system. This scan is named after the connect() call used by an operating system to initiate a TCP connection to a remote device. A TCP connect() scan uses a standard TCP connection to verify which ports are open. TCP connect() scans uses the same TCP handshake connection that other networked TCP-based applications use. This type of scan will be logged by the remote host and can be easily identified by an Intrusion Detection System or event log.

There are various scanning techniques to test for open ports on a remote system without being logged. One of these stealth techniques is the SYN scan, which is often referred to as "half open" scanning. A SYN scan uses standard methods of port-identification without completing the TCP handshake. As soon as an open port is identified, the TCP handshake is reset before it is completed. With a SYN scan, the host never actually creates a TCP session with a remote system. A SYN scan allows a remote system to be scanned without being logged.

The FIN, NULL or XMAS scans are often grouped together because of their similarities. These scans are stealthy because they send a single frame to a TCP port without any TCP handshaking or additional packet transfers. These scans send a single frame with the expectation of a single response. Sending these types of packets to a closed port will result in an RST response, while an open port will drop these packets. By identifying the closed ports, the open ports can then be extrapolated.

Nmap Introduction

Nmap is one of the industries' most complete free port scanners that is supported on Windows, Linux, Mac OS X, FreeBSD, OpenBSD, Solaris, HP-UX, NetBSD, Solaris, Amiga and more. Nmap is available from www.insecure.org at no cost under the terms of the GNU General Public License. Although there are countless commercial, Open Source, and gratis port scanners, I selected Nmap because of its performance, broad adoption and price.

On NIX and Windows platforms, Nmap can be executed from the command line or from a GUI interface called NmapFE. On the Windows platform, Nmap requires the WinPcap libraries; WinPcap requires administrative access to install. WinPcap can be downloaded from http://www.winpcap.org/. After WinPcap is installed on a Windows host, Nmap can be downloaded, unzipped to a directory, and executed from the directory via the command line.

Nmap allows us to run a wide variety of port scans and operating system identification scans using TCP/IP stack fingerprinting. Nmap interrogates a system's TCP/IP stack by sending the operating system different packets and then interpreting and reporting the response. The packets are specifically crafted to make the target operating system TCP/IP stack respond in a unique way. Knowing in advance how an

214

operating system TCP/IP stack will respond allows Nmap to determine relatively accurately which operating system the target system is running and its version number.

List 15.5 highlights Nmap's scanning capabilities:
- UDP, TCP connect()
- TCP SYN (half open)
- ftp proxy (bounce attack)
- ICMP (ping sweep)
- FIN, ACK sweep
- Xmas Tree,
- SYN sweep
- IP Protocol
- Null scan

Nmap also supports a wide variety of advanced scans.

List 15.6 highlights Nmap's advanced scanning capabilities:
- Stealth scanning
- Dynamic delay and retransmission calculations
- Parallel scanning
- Detection of down hosts via parallel pings
- Decoy scanning
- Port filtering detection
- Direct (non-portmapper) RPC scanning
- Fragmentation scanning
- Flexible target and port specification

On the NIX platform, root users enjoy full functionality in contrast to regular user access, which is slightly limited, in part because of the lack of many critical kernel interfaces, such as raw sockets (used for TCP/IP fingerprinting). A lot of effort has been put into Nmap to provide good performance for non-root users, although Nmap should be run as root whenever possible.

Nmap's Usage

Nmap can be used to scan a single host or an entire IP range, allowing detailed information to be obtained about a single host or all the hosts (routers, switches, hubs, firewalls, etc.) on a network. Nmap's results show a list of what is referred to as "interesting ports" on the system being scanned. Nmap always provides a port's service name, providing there is a service name, port number, state of the port (either open, filtered, unfiltered) and protocol.

List 15.7 shows the state of the port section of an Nmap scan:

- Open means that the target machine is accepting connections on that port.
- Filtered means that a firewall, some type of filter or other type of network barrier is obfuscating the port.
- Unfiltered means that Nmap knows that the port is closed and no firewall or filter is interfering. Unfiltered ports are very common and are exclusively shown when most of the scanned ports are in a filtered state.

Nmap supports fifteen separate scanning methods. Each scanning method has its own distinct characteristics, advantages and disadvantages. The majority of the scanning methods are straightforward and simple to execute, while others are more complex, requiring additional information be obtained before a scan can be executed.

The syntax of an Nmap scan is as follows:
nmap [Scan Type(s)] [Options] <host or net #1 ... [#N]>
The command "nmap" is what actually executes the scan. Multiple scan types and options can be combined to craft a scan.

List 15.8 shows a partial list of Scan Types:
- sS TCP SYN
- sT TCP connect() scan
- sF sX -sN Stealth FIN, Xmas Tree, or Null scan modes
- sP Ping scanning

List 15.9 shows a partial list of Options:
- P0 Do not try to ping hosts (ICMP) at all before scanning them (it is a Zero).
- PE This option uses a true ping (ICMP echo request) packet.

- O This option activates remote host identification via TCP/IP fingerprinting.
- 6 This option enables IPv6 support.

Tip: The help menu can be accessed from the command line by typing nmap –help; or for an exhaustive list of scan types and options, refer to Nmap's man pages. On an NIX system, man pages can be accessed by typing "man nmap" within a terminal window.

Next will be a walk through of an example scan to determine if the server role is properly configured. The scan will be executed against an individual Terminal Server to audit which services it offers, and will then use the netstat and tasklist commands to map executables to open ports. The goal of the example is to show how Nmap assists to quickly discover improperly configured and non-compliant computers or devices on a network.

Please Note: Never run scanners without explicit permission (preferably written) from your employer. Auditors and network and security administrators with the best intentions have been fired for running scanners without proper authority to do so.

The first example shows a TCP SYN scan (-sS option) with the -O (OS detection) option executed against a single Terminal Server host:

[root@sffc6mtv00 ~]# nmap -sS -O 192.168.1.203
Starting Nmap 4.11 (http://www.insecure.org/nmap/) at 2006-12-11 20:13 PST
Interesting ports on 192.168.1.203:
Not shown: 1674 closed ports
PORT   STATE SERVICE
135/tcp open msrpc
139/tcp open netbios-ssn
445/tcp open microsoft-ds
1025/tcp open NFS-or-IIS
1050/tcp open java-or-OTGfileshare
3389/tcp open ms-term-serv
MAC Address: 00:0C:29:7F:4F:13 (VMware)
Device type: general purpose
Running: Microsoft Windows 2003/.NET

OS details: Microsoft Windows Server 2003SP1
Nmap finished: 1 IP address (1 host up) scanned in 2.183 seconds
[root@sffc6mtv00 ~]#

The result from the example shows that ports 135/tcp, 139/tcp, 445/tcp, 1025/tcp, 1050/tcp, and 3389/tcp are open on the Terminal Server. The open ports confirm the Terminal Server role is properly configured. Ports 135/tcp, 139/tcp, 1025/tcp, and 1050/tcp are needed for intra machine communication. Port 3389/tcp is Terminal Services and port 445/tcp enables file and printer sharing. Port 445/tcp is the only port that could be disabled by disabling File and Printer Sharing for Microsoft Networks in the network adapters' properties. Let's review the example in greater detail.

Table 15.1 shows the scan line by line.

Table 15.1

Scan Output	Explanation
# nmap -sS -O 192.168.1.203	The command "nmap" invokes the scan, and the option -sS –O runs a TCP SYN scan with OS detection.
Starting Nmap 4.11 (http://www.insecure.org/nmap/) at 2006-12-11 20:13 PST	This indicates the time and date when the scan was run.
Interesting ports on 192.168.1.203:	This shows the IP address of the target machine.
Not shown: 1674 closed ports	This indicates the number of closed not shown ports.
PORT STATE SERVICE	This heading shows the PORT, STATE (state is either open, closed, filtered, or unfiltered) as well as the SERVICE.
135/tcp open msrpc	Microsoft RPC Locator Service.
139/tcp open netbios-ssn	NetBIOS Session Service.
445/tcp open microsoft-ds	SMB Direct / Microsoft-DS (Active Directory, Windows

	shares.)
1025/tcp open NFS-or-IIS	The lsass.exe process. It is responsible for management of local security authority domain authentication and Active Directory management.
1050/tcp open java-or-OTGfileshare	The svchost.exe process. It is a system process that handles processes executed from DLLs.
3389/tcp open ms-term-serv	Microsoft Terminal Services (RDP) officially registered as Windows Based Terminal (WBT).
MAC Address: 00:0C:29:7F:4F:13 (VMware)	Shows the MAC address.
Device type: general purpose	Indicates the device type as general purpose.
Running: Microsoft Windows 2003/.NET	Indicates the OS version.
OS details: Microsoft Windows Server 2003SP1	Indicates the OS version and SP level.
Nmap finished: 1 IP address (1 host up) scanned in 2.183 seconds	Shows that Nmap scanned one address in 2.183 seconds.

In many cases we need to know exactly which service is listening on a port in order to determine if it can be disabled, such as ports 1025/tcp and 1050/tcp from the last example. Determining exactly which service is listening on a port can be accomplished using the netstat -ano command to enumerate all of the running network services with their associated process identifier (PID) and the tasklist command to display the translation between PID and executable names.

The next example shows the result from netstat -ano on the same Terminal Server as in the first example. The output is truncated to save space.

C:\>netstat -ano
Active Connections

Proto	Local Address	Foreign Address	State	PID
TCP	0.0.0.0:1025	0.0.0.0:0	LISTENING	748
TCP	0.0.0.0:1050	0.0.0.0:0	LISTENING	144

Note ports 1025/tcp PID 748 and 1050/tcp PID 144. Next the tasklist command is executed to display the translation between process identifiers and executable names. The output is truncated to save space.

C:\>tasklist

Image Name	PID Session Name	Session#	Mem Usage
lsass.exe	748 RDP-Tcp#3	0	3,848 K
svchost.exe	144 RDP-Tcp#3	0	2,448 K

The result from the tasklist command shows that the lsass.exe executable is bound to port 1025/tcp and that svchost.exe is bound to 1050/tcp. Lsass.exe is a system process of the Microsoft Windows security mechanisms that specifically deals with local security and login policies. Svchost.exe is a system process belonging to the Microsoft Windows Operating System, which handles processes executed from DLLs.

Using the netstat -ano and tasklist commands allow precise identification of which executables are bound to a port. Identifying which executables are bound to a port comes in handy in trying to identify Registered Ports, Dynamic and/or Private Ports and random RPC Ports.

Nmap is an extremely useful tool that allows the scanning of individual servers and networks to determine which hosts are up and what ports they are listening on. The information gathered from Nmap scans allows the auditing of systems in order to validate if they are correctly configured by identifying what is running on a system.

Chapter 15 Summary

This chapter discussed Terminal Server system auditing. The chapter began with an introduction of pre- and post-auditing strategies and ended with an overview of Microsoft Baseline Security Analyzer, including an example scan against a Terminal Server. Next port scanning techniques were reviewed, followed by a review of Nmap and its usage, including an example scan against a Terminal Server.

Pre- and Post-Production Auditing
- All production servers should undergo regular security audits to ensure compliance with security policies and regulatory mandates.
- Pre- and post-production audits validate that a server is configured to specifications by eliminating possible security holes and missing hotfixes or patches.
- All servers should undergo pre-production audits, whereas the frequency of production audits depends on business and regulatory requirements.

Microsoft Baseline Security Analyzer
- Microsoft Baseline Security Analyzer is a tool to help determine the security posture of Windows servers as well as many other Microsoft products.
- The results of a Microsoft Baseline Security Analyzer scan include Microsoft's security recommendations and presents detailed remediation steps.
- Microsoft Baseline Security Analyzer is built on the Windows Update Agent and Microsoft Update infrastructure and supports Windows NT 4.0 SP4 or above, Windows 2000, Windows XP, Windows Server 2003, IIS 4.0 or above, SQL 7.0 and above, and Office 2000 and above.
- To run the Microsoft Baseline Security Analyzer, you must have local administrator rights to the computer you want to scan. Remote scans will require the Remote Registry service to be running.

Port Scanning Techniques

- Scanning software allows the creation and transmission of basic TCP/IP packets and sequences and unusual TCP/IP packets and sequences.
- Basic scanning techniques are logged by the remote host and can be easily identified by an Intrusion Detection System.
- A TCP connect() scan uses a standard TCP connection to verify which ports are open. This type of scan will be logged by the remote host and can be easily identified by an Intrusion Detection System or an event log.
- Stealth scanning techniques allow unusual TCP/IP packets and sequences that can go undetected on a remote system or identified by an Intrusion Detection System.
- A SYN scan uses standard methods of port-identification without completing the TCP handshake. As soon as an open port is identified, the TCP handshake is reset before it is completed. A SYN scan allows a remote system to be scanned without being logged.
- FIN, NULL or XMAS scans are often grouped together because of their similarities: they are stealthy because they send a single frame to a TCP port without any TCP handshaking or additional packet transfers.

Nmap

- Nmap is one of the industries' most complete free port scanners that is supported on Windows, Linux, Mac OS X, FreeBSD, OpenBSD, Solaris, HP-UX, NetBSD, Solaris, Amiga and more.
- Nmap runs a wide variety of port scans and operating system identification using TCP/IP stack fingerprinting.
- Nmap interrogates a system's TCP/IP stack by sending the operating system different packets and then interpreting and reporting the response.
- Nmap can be used to scan a single host or an entire IP range, to obtain detailed information about a single host or all the hosts (routers, switches, hubs, firewalls, etc.) on a network.
- Nmap's results show a list of what is referred to as "interesting ports" on the system being scanned.

- Nmap always provides a port's service name providing there is a service name, port number, and state of the port (either open, filtered, unfiltered) and protocol.

Netstat and tasklist
- The netstat -ano command will enumerate all of the running network services with their associated process identifier (PID).
- The tasklist command will displays the translation between PID and executable names.
- Using the netstat -ano command together with the tasklist command allows the precise identification of which executables are bound to a port.

The next chapter will introduce security log management strategies.

References:
TCP/IP stack fingerprinting written by Fyodor
http://www.insecure.org/nmap/nmap-fingerprinting-article.html

Chapter 16: Log Management Policy

Chapter Overview:

This chapter begins with a high level introduction of log management, Windows security logs and audit policies, followed with an overview of security event log monitoring. The chapter concludes with an example Log Management Policy. Log Management is a field unto itself and an exhaustive review is beyond the scope of this book. This chapter provides a high level introduction to log management, offers additional resources and focuses on Terminal Server log data and analysis and how to detect security and policy violations.

Log Management Introduction

Logs are records of events that occur within the information systems of an organization. Virtually every system, service, application and device in the Enterprise has built in logging capabilities. Originally log data was used to troubleshoot systems; but as systems and business requirements evolved, so did logging capabilities and log analysis. In today's Enterprise, logs are an invaluable resource used to optimize systems and networks, establish baselines, perform audits and assist with regulatory compliance. From a security perspective, log data along with intrusion detection systems (IDS) provides a wealth of information to identify security events, detect an attack in progress and analyze the results of security events.

System logs for operating systems and services, such as authentication, file and print, Terminal Server, DNS, email, and so forth, generate detailed information about their activity. Application logs have the ability to generate an audit trail of past transactions with time stamps, user names and object access details. Most network gear, such as firewalls, routers, switches, and so forth, have the ability to generate log data about their activity. Change management logs document all changes made to technologies within the Enterprise. Other types of logs, such as surveillance or physical access logs, provide detailed physical access audit trails. Each of these logs sources are an integral part of their respective administrators' jobs because the collection and analysis of the log data is one of their responsibilities.

In conjunction with the appropriate tools and procedures, audit trails can validate individual accountability, a way to reconstruct events, detect intrusions, identify problems and demonstrate regulatory compliance. The need to audit individual accountability, reconstruct events, detect intrusions, identify problems and demonstrate regulatory compliance emphasizes the need for organizations to develop an effective log management strategy to generate, analyze, store and dispose of log data.

To establish an effective log management strategy, organizations develop log management practices. Policies are used to define log management activities that support business objectives and regulatory mandates that cover log generation, analysis, transmission, storage, retention and disposal. A log management infrastructure provides Enterprise wide management of log records.

List 16.1 shows the scope of a log management infrastructure:
- Define a method to move logs into the infrastructure.
- Define a secure storage format for logs.
- Define log retention policies.
- Define approved access methods to logs.
- Define analysis tools to enable analysis among multiple log sources.
- Define processes to use log data as evidence in legal proceedings.

Log Generation, Analysis, Transmission, Storage, Retention & Disposal

One of the keys to effective log generation is to ensure that log data is indeed reported in event logs. For example, prior to Windows 2003 Server, all nine auditing categories were disabled by default which produced empty security logs. Windows 2003 Server has six of the nine auditing categories enabled by default, although they only audit for successful security events which may not satisfy business or regulatory objectives. To ensure effective log generation, organizations must carefully evaluate each system, application and device within the Enterprise to ensure that they are properly configured to generate log data.

In terms of log analysis, processes should be in place to define the frequency and who analyzes the log data. Periodic analysis of log data will assist to identify and troubleshoot operational issues and security events. Countless commercial and Open Source tools are available to help to analyze log data. Organizations need to review their unique security and log analysis requirements to select a solution that meets their objects.

Log transmission, storage and disposal are important considerations for a log management infrastructure to protect the confidentiality, integrity and availability of logs. Some logs are created for local storage or put in a file that is intended to be transmitted to another system for processing. Logs will inevitably be transmitted over the network from the host to the log infrastructure for processing, storage and disposal. Business and regulatory requirements will help determine log transmission, storage and disposal requirements.

Finally, log retention periods are a serious consideration that depends on each organization's individual requirements. If the log infrastructure is designed for troubleshooting and short-term reporting, a short retention period of one or two months may suffice. However, if the goal is regulatory compliance and/or legal obligations, log data may need to be stored for a number of years for auditing purposes. Incidentally, seven years is becoming a generally accepted timeframe for log data retention.

Tip: NIST Special Publication 800-92, entitled "Guide to Computer Security Log Management" is a 72-paged publication intended to assist organizations in understanding the need for sound computer security log management. It is considered a core resource for developing a log management infrastructure. Also the NIST Handbook's Chapter 18 offers guidance with audit trails.

Windows Security Logs & Audit Policies
Windows 2000 Server and Windows 2003 Server have three discrete event logs: Application, Security and System. The Application and

System logs are continually logging activities that occur on the server and the Security log records audit events. Windows 2000 Server disabled security logging by default, which generated empty security logs. Windows 2003 Server has six of the nine auditing categories enabled by default to audit only for successful security events. Event logs are stored locally on each host and there is no built-in method to centralize log management or reporting.

Security logs are dependent on Windows' audit policies. Audit policies need to be enabled on machines to capture security log data. Audit policies can be configured locally or centrally via Group Policy. Both methods accomplish the same goal, although using Group Policy is preferred because of its centralized configuration capabilities. After an audit policy is enabled, discrete log entries are generated with their associated event IDs. Event IDs provide information about an event that can be used to analyze log entries and generate reports. Security logs and event IDs are viewed with the Windows Event Viewer (eventvwr.msc).

To enable audit policies locally or to view a computer's effective audit policies, the Local Security Policy Console (secpol.msc) is the appropriate tool. From the Local Security Policy Console navigate to Security Settings > Local Policies > Audit Policy to view or enable audit policies. To configure audit policies using Group Policy, open the desired Group Policy Object and navigate to: Computer Configuration > Windows Settings > Security Settings > Local Policies > Audit Policy. A total of nine audit policies can be enabled to audit for successes, failures, or not audit the event at all.

Table 16.1 lists the Windows 2003 Server audit policies.

Table 16.1

Audit Policy	Explanation
Audit account logon events	This policy enables logging of login requests to a domain controller (AD) or local account (SAM). Default Setting: Success.
Audit account management	This policy enables logging of user or group modifications including creation, modification and deletion of an account, disabling or enabling an account,

	and password changes. Default Setting: • Success on domain controllers. • No auditing on member servers.
Audit directory service access	This policy enables logging of Active Directory object access, including Organizational Units, user accounts, group accounts, and Group Policy Objects. This policy tracks the same actions as the Audit account management policy at a more detailed level. Default Setting: • Success on domain controllers. • Undefined for a member computer.
Audit logon events	This policy enables logging of all logons and logoffs to a local computer (SAM) or domain controller (AD), either interactive or via the network. These events are logged where the logon event occurs. Default Setting: Success.
Audit object access	This policy enables logging of access to files, folders, registry keys, printers, and services, if the auditing settings, such as Security Audit Control List (SACL), are set on the objects themselves. Default Setting: No auditing.
Audit policy change	This policy enables logging of changes made to a local system's security policies and on domain controllers, tracks changes made to trust relationships. Default Setting: • Success on domain controllers. • No auditing on member servers.
Audit privilege use	This policy enables logging when user privileges are invoked on a computer. Enabling this policy can generate multiple events per use of privilege. An example is logging on locally, backing up files and folders, changing the system time, etc. Default Setting: No auditing.
Audit process tracking	This policy enables logging of process creation and exit and access to objects. An example is executing an application which would create numerous events for the running processes. This setting is typically only enabled

	in a development environment for debugging. Default Setting: No auditing.
Audit system events	This policy enables logging of events triggered by the computer, such as startup and shutdown events, loading of authentication packages, clearing of the audit log, and changes to the system time. Default Setting: <ul><li>Success on domain controllers.</li><li>No auditing on member servers.</li></ul>

As mentioned above, once an audit policy is enabled, discrete log entries are recorded with associated event IDs. Each audit policy event has event IDs that directly correlate to the event which can be used for analysis and reporting.

Individual objects can be audited and recorded in the security log by editing the System Access Control List (SACL) for the desired object. Editing the System Access Control List is similar to assigning file level permissions, except this configuration tells the operating system what type of object access will generate an event log entry. An object's System Access Control List can be modified by clicking the Advanced button on the Security tab from the object's properties. On the Auditing tab, click **Add** to include new auditing events for an object or click **View/Edit** to modify an existing auditing event.

The configurations of audit policies and individual object auditing should be governed by policy. Regulatory and business requirements need to be considered to determine which audit policies help meet objectives. A risk assessment could assist to identify the appropriate auditing requirements.

Event Log Settings
Both audit policies and event log setting can be configured locally or centrally via Group Policy. Event log settings allow the configuration of how the Security, Application and System logs behave. Attributes such as maximum log size, access rights and retention settings can be configured. The policies can be edited from the Default Domain Policy in the Computer Configuration > Windows Settings > Security Settings > Local Policies > Event Log section. To configure the

settings locally, open Windows Event Viewer (eventvwr.msc) and then right-click each log individually to access and edit their properties. It is possible to configure the log size, including the maximum size and the actions the operating system should take when that limit is reached.

List 16.2 shows the Group Policies used to configure event log settings:
- Maximum application log size
- Maximum security log size
- Maximum system log size
- Prevent local guests group from accessing application log
- Prevent local guests group from accessing security log
- Prevent local guests group from accessing system log
- Retain application log
- Retain security log
- Retain system log
- Retention method for application log
- Retention method for security log
- Retention method for system log

Event log settings should be governed by Enterprise Architecture policy. Many of the event log settings would be defined within the log management infrastructure's layered policies or within general organizational policy. For example, a Retention Policy would provide guidance for many log settings. An organization's regulatory and business objectives would dictate the appropriate event log settings. A risk assessment could assist in determining the requirements.

Security Event Log Monitoring & Terminal Server
Investigating security events within a Terminal Server environment can be a very challenging task because there may be a need to sift through megabytes and sometimes gigabytes of log data spread through the Enterprise. When a security event occurs, many times there is simply too much data to review to make sense of what happened. Organizations turn to Intrusion Detection Systems to monitor network traffic for suspicious activity and security information and event management systems (SIEM) to manage their log infrastructure. Security information event management systems,

and log management tools offer centralization, sorting and parsing of log file data. Countless commercial and Open Source solutions are available to meet any organization's requirements. Regardless of which solution(s) an organization uses, security log management analysis practices are identical, such as the ability to identify, contain and respond quickly to security events in the network.

One of the primary goals of security log monitoring is to detect suspicious activity and audit systems for compliance. Within a Terminal Server environment, log data can be leveraged to detect a wide variety of suspicious activity such as: brute force attacks, authentication failures, account lockouts, successful and unsuccessful file access attempts, unexpected system shutdowns and attempts to tamper with event logs.

Note: When processing any log files to ensure the credibility of the log files, it is important to work on copies of the logs to preserve the integrity of the original files.

The following sections will overview brute force attacks, tracking authentication failures, account lockouts, unsuccessful and successful file access attempts, system shutdowns and attempts to tamper with event logs.

Brute Force Attacks

Chapter 7 reviewed brute force attacks and it was learned that intruders use two key technical methods to obtain passwords: brute-force and dictionary attacks. A brute force attack enters every possible combination of characters and numbers until the machine accepts one of the combinations as the correct password. A dictionary attack enters each word in the dictionary to guess the correct password. Both of these attacks have the same signature: one failed event after another, another, and another. This type of attack signature is a brute force attack.

In Terminal Server environments, this type of attack is typically perpetrated against administrator accounts that cannot be locked out with an account lockout policy. One approach to protect the administrator account from a brute force attack is to rename it. User accounts are protected against brute force attacks by employing account lockout policies that disable an account after a defined number of incorrect password attempts. Account lockouts can be configured to last a specific duration, configured in minutes, or configured to remain locked until manually unlocked by an administrator. An account lockout policy is typically employed by organization to protect user accounts within their firewall. Remote access or web access requires unique attention because account lockout policies can be exploited to lock out user accounts, causing denial of service. Some web sites are unable to enforce a lockout policy because they would continually be unlocking customer accounts.

There are two Windows audit policies, when enabled and configured, that record failed events and assist to detect brute force attacks: Audit Account Logon Events and Audit Logon Events.

List 16.3 highlights each policy.
- Audit Account Logon Events
  - On domain controllers, the policy records all log on or off attempts with a domain user account. The events are logged in the domain controller's security log. On a workstation or member server, the policy records all log on or off attempts with a local account. The event is logged locally in the host's security log. The policy can be configured to audit successes, audit failures, or not audit the event at all. Success audits record an entry when an account logon attempt succeeds. Failure audits record an entry when an account logon attempt fails.

- Audit Logon Events
  - On domain controllers, the policy records attempts to log on or off the domain controller. On a workstation or member server, the policy records all attempts to log on or off the local computer, with a domain account or a local account. The policy can be configured to audit successes, audit failures, or not audit the event at all. Success audits record an entry when an account logon attempt succeeds. Failure audits record an entry when an account logon attempt fails.

The primary differences between the two policies is that the Audit logon events can be used to associate process tracking and object access events to a logon session. It also records more granular details about the logon type, failed logons and logoffs than the Audit Account Logon Events policy. If the goal is to audit all domain account authentication, the Audit account logon events is the preferred policy.

A security information and event management system, log management tool or the Windows Event Viewer could be used to identify a brute force attack by parsing Windows security logs for the following event IDs; 529, 530, 531, 532, 533, 534, 535, 537 and 539.

Table 16.2 lists the event IDs.

Table 16.2

Event ID	Type	Description
529	Failure	Logon Failure: Unknown user name or bad password.
530	Failure	Logon Failure: *Account logon time restriction violation.
531	Failure	Logon Failure: The specified user account is currently disabled.
532	Failure	Logon Failure: *The specified user account has expired.
533	Failure	Logon Failure: *User not allowed to log on at this computer.
534	Failure	Logon Failure: The requested logon type is not permitted.
535	Failure	Logon Failure: The specified account password has expired.
537	Failure	Logon Failure: An unexpected error occurred during logon.
539	Failure	Logon Failure: The specified user account is locked out.

* Applies only to Domain Accounts

Tracking Authentication Failures

Tracking authentication failures is an important part of regular system audits. It allows administrators to identify intrusion attempts, determine which users are experiencing isolated or repeated authentication problems, find users that are locked out and troubleshot authentication issues.

The audit policy settings and event IDs used to detect brute force attacks are identical to track authentication failures. The difference between a brute force attack and an authentication failure is the attack signature, such as the number and frequency of failed authentications. A brute force attack signature has a very high number of authentication failures in contrast to a user authentication failure which typically has a much lower number and frequency of failed authentications.

Account Lockouts

As reviewed in the Brute Force Attacks section, the account lockout policy controls what happens to an account after a defined number of incorrect password attempts. Auditing for account lockouts is an important part of regular system audits, providing detailed account lockout metrics used to track user account lockouts or brute force attacks.

There are three Windows audit policies that assist in detecting account lockouts: Audit Account Logon Events, Audit Account Management, and Audit Logon Events.

List 16.4 shows the policies and settings to track account lockouts.
- Audit Account Logon Events - Failure
- Audit Account Management Events - Success
- Audit Logon Events - Failure

The Audit Account Management Events policy is used to record changes to user accounts, groups and logs password resets, newly created accounts and changes to group membership. For domain controllers, the policy records changes to domain users, domain groups and computer accounts. On a workstation or member server, the policy records changes to local users and groups. The policy is useful in auditing account management activities by administrators, Help desk personnel or intruders.

A security information and event management system, log management tool or the Windows Event Viewer could be used to identify account lockouts by looking in the Windows security logs for the following event IDs: 529, 644, 675.

Table 16.3 lists the event IDs.

Table 16.3

Event ID	Type	Description
529	Failure	Logon Failure: Unknown user name or bad password. This event can help identify the source of the lockout.
644	Failure	Indicates that the account is locked out.
675	Failure	Pre-authentication failed. This event is generated on a Key Distribution Center (KDC) when a user types in an incorrect password. This event can help identify the source of the lockout.

Successful and Unsuccessful File Access Attempts

Auditing for successful and unsuccessful file access attempts can be an important part of system audits by providing records of who accessed or tried to access data. Auditing for successful and unsuccessful file access attempts is also especially helpful to comply with regulatory mandates by providing an audit trail of who accessed critical data.

Auditing files requires an NTFS file system (NT file system) to enable auditing at the file system level or on directories or individual files. Once enabled, successful and unsuccessful access attempts will be recorded in the security event log. Enabling NTFS object auditing allows auditors and administrators to determine who successfully and or unsuccessfully accessed the audited NTFS object. Note that NTFS object auditing can generate substantial quantities of log data. If used generously, it will quickly fill up the security event log.

A security information and event management system, log management tool or the Windows Event Viewer could be used to identify successful and unsuccessful file access attempts by looking in the Windows security logs for event ID 560.

Table 16.4 shows event ID 560.

Table 16.4

Event ID	Type	Description
560	Success Failure	Object open

Unexpected System Shutdowns

When an unexpected system shutdown occurs, the target system needs to be evaluated to determine the root cause of the system shutdown to prevent additional outages. A system shutdown will generate a log entry in the system log with event ID 6008. Unlike the other examples in this chapter, this event does not require an audit policy because it is generated by default. Power failures, viruses, operating system crashes and human error are a short list of some of the causes of unexpected system showdowns. Many popular tools are available on the Internet that can be used to reset the local or domain administrator's password by booting a server from a floppy or CDROM. The availability of password reset tools emphasizes the need to enforce physical security controls along with monitoring of unexpected system shutdowns.

A security information and event management system, log management tool or the Windows Event Viewer can be used to identify an unexpected system shutdown by looking in the Windows system logs for event ID 6008.

Table 16.5 shows event ID 6008.

Table 16.5

Event ID	Type	Description
6008	Warning	The previous system shutdown at <time> on <date> was unexpected.

Attempts to Tamper with Event Logs

Detecting event log tampering is an important part of system audits in order to ensure the confidentially, integrity and availability of log data. If an intruder, disgruntled employee or rouge administrator compromises a system, they may try to hide their tracks by tampering with or destroying log data. The Windows System Event logs events to help detect tampering with or destroying log data.

A security information and event management system, log management tool or the Windows Event Viewer could be used to detect tampering with or destroying log data by looking in the Windows System Event logs for event ID 512 and 517.

Table 16.6 shows event ID 512 and 517.

Table 16.6

Event ID	Type	Description
512	Success	Indicated that the system is starting up. If the physical security of a machine is compromised, a system is particularly vulnerable during a system restart.
517	Success	Indicated that the audit log was cleared. It will log the following details: Primary User Name: <user name> Primary Domain: <domain name> Primary Logon ID: <logon id> Client User Name: <client user name> Client Domain: <domain> Client Logon ID: <logon id>

The following tier 2 Log Management Policy defines an organization's requirements in term of log management. The example policy starts with a Purpose and Scope statement and then proceeds with the policy. This policy is intended for informational purposes only.

Log Management Policy

Purpose
This purpose of this policy is to define <Company Name>'s log management practices and requirements in terms of log generation, log formats, log storage, log transmission, log access, log analysis, log retention and log disposal.

Scope
This policy applies to all <Company Name>'s Application Logs, System Logs, Network Logs, Change Management Logs, Physical Access Logs and Surveillance Logs.

Policy
<Company Name>'s log management practice encompasses the following:
- Defines log generation requirements.
- Defines log format requirements.
- Defines log transport requirements.
- Defines log storage requirements.
- Defines log access requirements.
- Defines log analysis tool requirements.
- Defines log retention requirements.
- Defines log disposal requirements.

Log Generation Requirements
- Application Logs

Applications should have the capability to record their activity to support business processes and regulatory mandates.

- System Logs

System logs are generated from a wide variety of sources. Example sources of system logs are operating systems, authentication servers, database servers, web servers, print servers, file servers, DHCP servers, DNS and email servers. System logs should be capable of recording the following:

- o Record requested operations.
- o Record whether the request was accepted or denied.
- o Record the time and date the operation was performed.
- o Record who and/or what system initiated the operation.
- o Record system and network resources used.

- Network Logs

Network logs are generated from a wide variety of sources. Example sources of network logs are routers, switches, intrusion detection and prevention systems, wireless access points, network based firewalls, host based firewalls and telephone switches. Network logs should record the following:

- o Record the IP addresses or telephone numbers of the end points.
- o Record the port numbers for each of the end points.
- o Record whether connections where accepted or denied.
- o Record the date, time and duration of connections.
- o Record the number of packets and bytes of traffic.

- Change Management Logs

Change Management Logs are governed by the Change Management Policy.

- Physical and Surveillance Access Logs

Physical and Surveillance Access Logs are governed by the Environmental Controls Policy.

Log Format Requirements

Logs will be archived in a standard format.

Log Transport Requirements

Logs will traverse the network in encrypted format.

Log Storage Requirements

Logs will be stored in a secured centralized repository.

Log Access Requirements
Logs will be view exclusively by approved personnel.

Log Analysis Requirements
Logs analysis tools will parse records from multiple sources and protect the original log data in the event log records are used in legal proceedings.

Log Retention Requirements
Log retention requirements are governed by the Record Retention Policy.

Log Disposal Requirements
Log Disposal requirements are governed by the Media Sanitization Policy.

Policy Review
This policy will be reviewed annually.

Compliance
Any employee found to have violated this policy may be subject to disciplinary action, up to and including termination of employment.

Related Policies
Change Management Policy
Environmental Controls Policy
Record Retention Policy
Media Sanitization Policy

Reference
NIST Special Publication 800-92
NIST Handbook Chapter 18
ISO/IEC 17799 Section 10

Chapter 16 Summary

This chapter introduced log management and Windows security logs and audit policies and was followed with an overview of security event log monitoring. The chapter concluded with an example Log Management Policy.

Log Management Intro
- Logs are records of events that occur within an organization's information systems.
- Virtually every system, service, application and device in the Enterprise has built in logging capabilities.
- System logs for operating systems and services, such as authentication, file and print, Terminal Server, DNS, email, and so forth, generate detailed information about their activity.
- Application logs have the ability to generate an audit trail of past transactions with time stamps, user names and object access details.
- Most network gear, such as firewalls, routers and switches, have the ability to generate log data about their activity.
- Change management logs document all changes made to technologies within the Enterprise.
- Other types of logs, such as surveillance or physical access logs, provide detailed physical access audit trails.
- To establish an effective log management strategy, organizations develop log management practices.

Log Generation, Analysis, Transmission, Storage, Retention & Disposal
- One of the keys to effective log generation is to ensure that log data is indeed reported in event logs.
- In terms of log analysis, processes should be in place to define the frequency and who analyzes the log data.
- Periodic analysis of log data will assist in identifying and troubleshooting operational issues and security events.
- Log transmission, storage and disposal are important considerations for a log management infrastructure in order to protect the confidentiality, integrity and availability of logs.

- Logs will inevitably be transmitted over the network from the host to the log infrastructure for processing, storage and disposal.
- Business and regulatory requirements will help determine log transmission, storage retention and disposal requirements.
- NIST Special Publication 800-92, entitled "Guide to Computer Security Log Management," is a 72 page publication that is intended to assist organizations in understanding the need for sound computer security log management.

Windows Security Logs & Audit Policies
- Windows 2000 Server and Windows 2003 Server have three discrete event logs: Application, Security and System.
- The Application and System logs are continually logging activities that occur on the server and the Security log records audit events.
- Windows 2003 Server has six of the nine auditing categories enabled by default to audit only for successful security events.
- Event logs are stored locally on each host and there is no built-in method to centralize log management or reporting.
- Security logs are dependent on Windows audit policies. Audit policies need to be enabled on machines to capture security log data.
- Audit policies can be configuring locally or centrally via Group Policy.
- After an audit policy is enabled, discrete log entries are generated with their associated event IDs.
- Individual objects can be audited and recorded in the security log by editing the System Access Control List (SACL) for the desired object.

Event Log Settings
- Event log settings allow the configuration of how the Security, Application and System logs behave. Attributes such as maximum log size, access rights and retention settings can be configured.
- Event log settings should be governed by Enterprise Architecture policy. Many of the event log settings would be

defined within the log management infrastructure's layered policies or within general organizational policy.

Security Event Log Monitoring & Terminal Server

- When a security event occurs, often there is simply too much data to review to make sense of what happened. Organizations turn to Intrusion Detection Systems (IDS) to monitor network traffic for suspicious activity and security information and to event management (SIEM) systems to manage their log infrastructure.
- Security information and event management systems and log management tools offer centralization, sorting and parsing of log file data.
- One of the primary goals of security log monitoring is to detect suspicious activity and audit systems for compliance.
- Within a Terminal Server environment, log data can be leveraged to detect a wide variety of suspicious activity, such as brute force attacks, authentication failures, account lockouts, successful and unsuccessful file access attempts, unexpected system shutdowns and attempts to tamper with event logs.
- When processing any log files, to ensure the credibility of the log files, it is important to work on copies of the logs.

The next chapter will introduce incident response capabilities, followed with an example Incident Response Policy.

Reference:
NIST Special Publication 800-92
NIST Handbook Chapter 18
ISO/IEC 17799 Section 10

Chapter 17: Incident Response Policy

Chapter Overview:
This chapter reviews incident response capabilities and introduces an example Incident Response Policy. The chapter begins with a brief overview of incident response capabilities and an introduction to NIST Special Publication 800-61 and concludes with an example Incident Response Policy. Incident Response is a field unto itself and a detailed review of its principles, processes, and approach is beyond the scope of this book. This chapter shows the importance of incident response capabilities, introduces additional references and shows how Incident Response relates to Terminal Server.

Even with the most sophisticated, state of the art security systems and effective policies, security incidents will occur. The most common security incidents are viruses, malware, laptop theft and employee network abuse. Less common security events are denial of service attacks, sabotage, intellectual proprietary theft, fraud and system penetration from external sources. Sooner or later, every organization will need to respond to a security incident. A quick, well orchestrated response will minimize loss and damage; in contrast, a poor response could result in financial, legal, and public relations problems.

An Incident Response Policy is used to define how an organization responds to security incidents. It is an action oriented policy that is used to provide guidance to quickly detect security incidents, minimize loss, mitigate exploited weaknesses and rapidly restore services. The majority of the Enterprise Architecture policies reviewed in this book have been passive policies that provide guidance with appropriate systems usage, technology standards, system design, system configurations and auditing. An Incident Response Policy is an action oriented policy that requires quick and efficient execution in order to protect an organization's assets.

In regards to Terminal Server, security incidents typically occur within a Terminal Server user session. An example of some of the incidents that originate from Terminal Server user sessions are malware infection, network abuse, sabotage, intellectual proprietary theft and fraud. These types of security incidents are typically discovered by technical or administrative security control, an audit or an employee. When one of these security incidents is detected, an Incident Response Policy is the primary administrative control used to mitigate the damage.

Organizations that must comply with regulatory mandates must undergo regular audits to validate incident response capabilities. A number of widely adopted guidelines can be used to assist organizations in understanding how to implement incident response capabilities. Two examples of guidelines are ISO/IEC 17799 section 13 and NIST Special Publication 800-61.

The NIST Special Publication 800-61 is a free, 148-paged Computer Security Incident Handling Guide which contains eight chapters and ten appendixes. The goal of NIST Special Publication 800-61 is to assist organizations to establish computer security incident response capabilities. It is an in-depth document that is widely adopted and used in both the public and private sectors to implement incident response capabilities.

List 17.1 shows NIST Special Publication 800-61 areas of focus:
- Organizing a computer security incident response capability.
- Establishing incident response policies and procedures.
- Structuring an incident response team.
- Handling incidents from initial preparation through the post-incident lessons learned phase.
- Handling specific types of incidents.

The following Incident Response Policy defines how an organization responds to security incidents. The example policy starts with a Purpose and Scope statement and then proceeds with the policy. This policy is intended for informational purposes only.

246

Incident Response Policy

Purpose
This purpose of this policy is to define a formal reporting and response procedure to be followed when responding to security incidents. Implementing formal reporting and response procedures ensures that information security events are communicated in a manner allowing timely corrective action to be made while applying a consistent approach to the management of information security incidents.

Scope
This policy applies to all employees and non-employees working for or with <Company Name>.

Policy
A security incident is described as one or more of the following conditions:
- Any potential violation of Federal law, State law, or <Company Name> policy involving an Information Technology (IT) asset.
- A breach, attempted breach or other unauthorized access to <Company Name's> IT asset.
- Any Internet worm, virus, Denial of Service (DoS) attack or related incident.
- Any change in a computer system that disables or defeats security precautions.
- Any failure in network or computer systems that disrupts IT services.
- Any employee or non-employee who violates policy.

Reporting a Security Incident
Employees and non-employees working for or with <Company Name> will immediately report the following:
- A security incident that involves unauthorized physical access to a building or secure location, physical threat, imminent danger or personal safety issue.
- An actual or suspected security incident that involves unauthorized access to information systems, such as:

- o Malicious alteration or destruction of data, information or communications.
- o Unauthorized interception or monitoring of communications.
- o Any deliberate and unauthorized destruction or damage of IT resources.

Excluding the steps outlined below, it is essential that all investigative or corrective action be taken only by InfoSec personnel. When faced with a potential security incident, employees and non-employees should do the following if the incident involves a compromised computer system:

- Do not alter the state of the computer system.
- The computer system should remain on and all currently running computer programs should be left as is.
- Do not shutdown or restart the computer.
- Immediately disconnect the computer from the network by removing the cable from the back of the computer.
- Report the security incident to InfoSec.

InfoSec Contacts:
<Names and Phone Numbers>

Response
InfoSec staff will first determine if the Security Incident justifies a formal incident response. In cases where a Security Incident does not require an incident response, the situation will be forwarded to the appropriate area of operations to ensure that all technology support services required are rendered.

An incident response may range from getting a critical system back online, gathering evidence, taking appropriate legal action against individual(s), or in some cases notifying appropriate ISP's or other third parties of inappropriate activity originating from their network.

Any contacts or attempted contacts from the media regarding an incident should be redirected to the marketing/communication department.

Policy Review
This policy will be reviewed annually.

Compliance
Any employee found to have violated this policy may be subject to disciplinary action, up to and including termination of employment.

Reference
NIST Special Publication 800-61
NIST Handbook Chapter 12
ISO/IEC 17799 section 13

The example Incident Response Policy shows how a policy is used to define how an organization responds to security incidents.

Chapter 17 Summary
This chapter discussed incident response capabilities and concluded with an example Incident Response Policy.

- Even with the most sophisticated, state of the art security systems and effective policies, security incidents will occur.
- The most common security incidents are viruses, malware, laptop theft and employee network abuse.
- Less common security events are denial of service attacks, sabotage, intellectual proprietary theft, fraud and system penetration from external sources.
- Sooner or later, every organization will need to respond to a security incident. A quick, well orchestrated response will minimize loss and damage in contrast to a poor response that could result in financial and public relations problems.
- An Incident Response Policy is an action oriented policy that is used to provide guidance quickly to detect security incidents, minimize loss, mitigate exploited weaknesses and rapidly restore services.
- ISO/IEC 17799 section 13 and NIST Special Publication 800-61 provide guidance on how to implement incident response capabilities.

The next chapter will introduce Vulnerability Assessments and an example Audit Vulnerability Scan Policy.

Resources:
NIST Special Publication 800-61
ISO/IEC 17799 section 13
CERT® Coordination Center Incident Reporting Guidelines
http://www.cert.org/tech_tips/incident_reporting.html

Chapter 18: Audit Vulnerability Scan Policy

Chapter Overview:
This chapter begins with an overview of a Vulnerability Assessment, followed by an example tier 2 Audit Vulnerability Scan Policy. Vulnerability Assessments are an essential tool for determining the security posture of an Enterprise and are an integral part of a security program. Vulnerability Assessments can be performed in house or by an independent 3rd party. Many organizations choose to use both in order to gain a broader perspective of their security posture.

Please Note: Never perform a Vulnerability Assessment without explicit and preferably written permission from your employer. Network and security administrators with the best intentions have been fired for performing Vulnerability Assessment without proper authority to do so.

A Vulnerability Assessment is a technique of evaluating the security posture of an Enterprise or network using passive and active analysis of the target systems for known weaknesses, technical flaws, or vulnerabilities. Vulnerability Assessments provides a level of assurance that script kiddies, skilled intruders and malicious users cannot compromise an organization's systems. Vulnerability Assessments should be performed on all supporting computers and networking gear that touch the Terminal Server environment. It is not uncommon for organizations to perform a Vulnerability Assessment monthly or immediately after vulnerabilities are discovered or become publicized on the Internet. For example, if there is a mis-configured Terminal Server, it could be compromised by a well known vulnerability and used as a hacking vector to other systems behind the firewall.

The Vulnerability Assessment process involves passive and active analysis of the target systems for known weaknesses, technical flaws or vulnerabilities. All of the discovered security issues will be presented to the system owners, together with a detailed assessment of the impact and a proposal for mitigation.

Vulnerability Assessments follows the typical pattern that an intruder or malicious user would use to gain information about a target host or network. This first step starts with reconnaissance. Reconnaissance can be a quick ping sweep to see what IP addresses on the network respond; searching newsgroups on the Internet looking for ill-advised employees divulging useful information; or it can be dumpster diving to find useful information like passwords, employee names and contacts. Basic reconnaissance can be performed by visiting an organization's website and gathering as much information as possible about the company. Public websites generally yield a wide variety of information that could be used to exploit systems and trick employees. For example, many organizations list the names of their management team on their public website. This information can be used for a social engineering attack, allowing an attacker to call or email employees using the names of the management staff to trick an employee into giving the attacker valuable information. Many public websites provide hints as to the type of systems an organization uses, which can be used to craft an attack against known vulnerabilities. Other reconnaissance techniques include using publicly available tools, such as InterNIC (http://www.internic.net/) and ARIN (http://www.arin. net/), to collect additional information about the domain registrations. Reconnaissance can also include theft, deception, tapping phones and networks, impersonations, or even leveraging falsified relationships to gather data about a target. The search for information is only limited by the extremes an attacker is willing to go.

Note: Social engineering is a method used to obtain confidential information by manipulation and deception.

After an intruder has collected enough information, the next step is to scan the target organization's external facing systems or network for open ports and services. The scanning process can yield important information, such as ports open through the router and firewall, available services and applications on hosts' or network appliances, and possibly the version of the operation system or application. After an intruder has mapped out available hosts, ports, applications and services, the next step is to test for known vulnerabilities that might exist on a host or network. When vulnerabilities are discovered, attacks are crafted and launched against systems. If attackers are able to compromise a system and gain access, they do their thing (whatever that is), and then they try to cover their tracks and leave a back door.

List 18.1 shows the pattern an attacker uses to penetrate systems:
- Reconnaissance
- Scanning
- Craft an attack
- Cover their tracks

There are many reasons why an organization would choose to perform a Vulnerability Assessment.

List 18.2 highlights some of the reasons:
- Identify threats facing an organization's information assets so they can be quantified to produce a risk analysis.
- Provide an organization with assurances that they have a thorough and comprehensive assessment of their organizational security policies.
- Gain and maintain certification to industry regulations (BS7799, Sarbanes-Oxley, HIPAAA, etc).
- Adopt best practice by conforming to legal and industry regulations.

A Vulnerability Assessment involves the systematic analysis of an organization's IT portfolio. It is crucial to set expectations, scope the project and have the explicit permission from management to perform the Vulnerability Assessment. The exact requirements should be agreed upon in a formal document or Statement of Work (SOW) prior to starting the project.

The real value of a Vulnerability Assessment is in the final report and executive summaries that are delivered to management and system owners. The deliverables need to be clear and easy to understand. The reports and executive summaries should be broken into sections that specifically target their intended audience, i.e. management, system owners, and so forth. Non-technical stakeholders will need the risks and possible solutions clearly described in layman's terms; technical managers need a broad overview of the situation without being confused with too much detail; and system administrators need a host-by-host list of technical vulnerabilities to address.

List 18.3 shows the minimum deliverables of a Vulnerability Assessment:

- Executive summary.
- Detailed results of the testing performed.
- What the results indicate.
- Recommendations on types of corrective actions suggested.

The next example shows an Audit Vulnerability Scan Policy from the SANS Policy Project that defines the agreement to perform network security scanning. The example policy starts with a Purpose and Scope statement and then proceeds with the Policy. This policy is intended for informational purposes only.

Audit Vulnerability Scan Policy

Purpose
The purpose of this agreement is to set forth our agreement regarding network security scanning offered by the <Internal or External Audit Name> to the <Company Name>. <Internal or External Audit Name> shall utilize <Approved Name of Software> to perform electronic scans of Client's networks and/or firewalls or on any system at <Company Name>.

Audits may be conducted to:

- Ensure integrity, confidentiality and availability of information and resources.
- Investigate possible security incidents ensure conformance to <Company Name> security policies.
- Monitor user or system activity where appropriate.

Scope
This policy covers all computer and communication devices owned or operated by <Company Name>. This policy also covers any computer and communications device that are presently on <Company Name> premises, but which may not be owned or operated by <Company Name>. The <Internal or External Audit Name> will not perform Denial of Service activities.

Policy
When requested, and for the purpose of performing an audit, consent to access needed will be provided to members of <Internal or External Audit Name>. <Company Name> hereby provides its consent to allow <Internal or External Audit Name> to access its networks and/or firewalls to the extent necessary to allow [Audit organization] to perform the scans authorized in this agreement. <Company Name> shall provide protocols, addressing information and network connections sufficient for <Internal or External Audit Name> to utilize the software to perform network scanning.

This access may include:
- User level and/or system level access to any computing or communications device.
- Access to information (electronic, hardcopy, etc.) that may be produced, transmitted or stored on <Company Name> equipment or premises.
- Access to work areas (labs, offices, cubicles, storage areas, etc.).
- Access to interactively monitor and log traffic on <Company Name> networks.

Network Control
If Client does not control their network and/or Internet service is provided via a second or third party, these parties are required to approve scanning in writing if scanning is to occur outside of the <Company Name's> LAN. By signing this agreement, all involved parties acknowledge that they authorize <Internal or External Audit Name> to use their service networks as a gateway for the conduct of these tests during the dates and times specified.

Service Degradation and/or Interruption
Network performance and/or availability may be affected by the network scanning. <Company Name> releases <Internal or External Audit Name> of any and all liability for damages that may arise from network availability restrictions caused by the network scanning, unless such damages are the result of <Internal or External Audit Name>'s gross negligence or intentional misconduct.

Client Point of Contact during the Scanning Period
<Company Name> shall identify in writing a person to be available if the <Internal or External Audit Name> Scanning Team has questions regarding data discovered or requires assistance.

Scanning period
<Company Name> and <Internal or External Audit Name> Scanning Team shall identify in writing the allowable dates for the scan to take place.

Compliance
Any employee found to have violated this policy may be subject to disciplinary action, up to and including termination of employment.

The above Audit Vulnerability Scan Policy example shows how a policy can provide an organization with a strategy to engage in network security scanning.

Chapter 18 Summary
This chapter discussed Vulnerability Assessment and concluded with an example Audit Vulnerability Scan Policy.

- A Vulnerability Assessment is a technique of evaluating the security posture of an Enterprise or network by simulating a variety of known attacks.
- A Vulnerability Assessment provides a level of assurance that script kiddies, skilled intruders and malicious users cannot compromise an organization's systems.
- A Vulnerability Assessment should be performed on all systems, including computers, storage and networking gear.

- It is not uncommon for organizations to perform a Vulnerability Assessment monthly or immediately after vulnerabilities are discovered or become publicized on the Internet.
- The Vulnerability Assessment process involves passive and active analysis of the target systems for known weaknesses, technical flaws or vulnerabilities.
- A Vulnerability Assessment follows the typical pattern that an intruder or malicious user would use to gain information about a target host or network.
- The real value of a Vulnerability Assessment is in the final report and executive summaries that are delivered to management and system owners at the end.
- An organization's Enterprise Architecture should include policies on conducting a Vulnerability Assessment, such as an Audit Vulnerability Scan Policy.

Resources:
The SANS Policy Project
ISECOM - Institute for Security and Open Methodologies

Index

SECURING MICROSOFT TERMINAL SERVICES

Change Management Policy, 7, 80, 81, 82, 83, 134, 139, 145, 150, 172, 193, 195, 203, 240, 241
Change Request, 83
Classification, 6, 66, 67, 68, 69, 72, 75, 76, 85, 98, 103
Clearinghouse, 34, 40, 43
Client Compatible encryption, 24, 157
Client Devices, 133
Client Drives Mapping, 22
Client Encryption Level, 157
Client-server, 4, 19, 20, 30, 45, 46, 48, 49, 51, 52, 102
Clustering, 33, 42, 189
COM, 22, 156, 177, 213
Communication, 4, 32, 34, 42, 43, 46, 47, 48, 63, 64, 65, 90, 91, 101, 102, 122, 154, 218, 248, 255
Compartmentalization of Information, 87, 95, 96, 97, 98, 103, 104, 105, 106
Compliance, 1, 2, 3, 10, 11, 12, 13, 17, 63, 65, 72, 79, 83, 89, 90, 91, 95, 109, 110, 111, 112, 114, 115, 118, 119, 126, 127, 134, 137, 139, 141, 145, 149, 158, 160, 172, 174, 185, 187, 189, 193, 195, 196, 203, 205, 211, 212, 221, 225, 226, 227, 232, 241, 244, 249, 256
Components, 22, 25, 37, 38, 57, 73, 84, 154, 156, 157, 164, 165, 166, 167, 168, 169, 194
Compression, 75
Computing Models, 4, 16, 45, 51, 52
Connection, 21, 25, 32, 39, 41, 94, 133, 143, 165, 209, 213, 222
Control Framework, 3, 10, 12, 15, 17, 96, 110
Control Panel, 158, 170, 171, 174
Controlled, 37, 38, 41, 82, 92, 98, 99, 100, 125, 176, 181
COSO, 12, 17
CPU, 131
Criteria, 59, 63, 68, 85, 118, 179, 181
CRSS.EXE, 30

D

Data Storage Servers, 38, 40
Data/ Information Architecture Domain, 66, 84, 85
Debugging, 229

Defense in Depth, 67, 87, 95, 96, 103, 106, 107, 117, 147, 151
Deployment, 30, 37, 59, 60, 63, 75, 76, 85, 132, 134, 139, 141
Desktop, 3, 4, 5, 15, 16, 20, 21, 37, 48, 51, 61, 73, 75, 76, 86, 93, 122, 132, 133, 134, 135, 137, 146, 148, 151, 152, 158, 160, 166, 170, 171, 172, 173, 174, 176, 186, 187, 191, 192, 194, 200, 202, 210, 211
Desktops, 3, 5, 16, 59, 63, 85
Development Environment, 229
Disallowed, 177, 178, 181, 182, 183, 186, 188
Discovery, 34
Disposal, 139, 145, 226, 227, 239, 241, 242, 243
DMZ, 98, 100
DNS, 40, 101, 162, 165, 166, 197, 198, 200, 225, 240, 242
Domain Controller, 34, 131, 209, 228, 229, 230, 233, 235
Drive Mapping, 21, 143

E

Encryption, 24, 25, 29, 73, 80, 81, 104, 105, 119, 125, 156, 157, 159
Engineering, 120, 121, 124, 126, 252
Enterprise Architecture, 3, 5, 6, 11, 15, 16, 55, 56, 57, 58, 59, 84, 87, 95, 96, 106, 109, 117, 211, 231, 243, 245, 257
Enterprise Security Architecture, 4, 16, 86, 87, 95, 96, 99, 106, 107
Enterprise Security Policy, 7, 87, 90, 95, 106, 117
Environmental, 8, 81, 109, 110, 112, 114, 240, 241
Error, 26, 97, 234, 237
Evaluating, 251, 256
Event Log, 143, 213, 222, 225, 226, 227, 230, 231, 236, 238, 242, 243, 244
Events, 70, 154, 225, 226, 227, 228, 229, 230, 231, 233, 234, 235, 238, 242, 243, 245, 247, 249
Eventvwr.msc, 228, 231
Exploit, 252

F

Facilities, 109, 114

260

Q

R

S

www.ingramcontent.com/pod-product-compliance
Lightning Source LLC
Chambersburg PA
CBHW021553210326
41599CB00010B/424